Your Wow Years

Your Wow Years

Supercharge the Second Half of Life

by Rita Connor

Your Wow Years: Supercharge the Second Half of Life
©2019 by Rita Connor

Printed in the United States of America.

eBook ISBN: 978-1-950370-06-1
Print ISBN: 978-1-950370-05-4
Library of Congress Control Number: 2019933858

Rita@YourWowYears.com
www.YourWowYears.com

 Published by Silver Torch Press
www.SilverTorchPress.com
Jill@SilverTorchPress.com

Dedication

To my loving family for all their wonderful support over the years.

If my dear friend and mentor, author Diana Loomans, hadn't said, "Rita, I think you have a book in you!" I am not sure I would be on this path!

To Kim O'Hara (of A Story Inside) for her excellent coaching as I wrote this book and to my fellow life travelers entering or living their precious second half of life: my greatest dream is for you to thrive and live the very best version of yourself in Your Wow Years!

Acknowledgements

I'd like to thank my supportive friends and family who encouraged me and said it was time to share my voice.

I'm thankful to my parents, Dr. John F. Connor M.D., and my mother, Moira Connor, for inspiring me to write. My father paved the way by writing seven volumes of "World War II As I Saw It" in the last 15 years of his life. My mother was an avid, lively letter writer who always encouraged me and was one of my biggest cheerleaders.

I thank Diana Loomans for her constant guidance and support in her Genius Writers classes, Kim O'Hara of A Story Inside for diligently reading and editing my manuscript for eight months, my fellow writer friends (Mai Lai Breech, Charlene Young, Gwen Matos, Susan Sherrard, Peter McGugan) and my siblings (John, Jo, Shirley, Michael, Moira, Jackie and Patrick) for all their encouragement.

Special thanks to Jill Fagan, everyone on the Silver Torch Press publishing team, and Cat Landry, my book cover designer.

Table of Contents

Foreword

I met Rita Connor when she was the president of Elite Resorts & Spas in 2008, representing several of the Joie de Vivre hotels and resorts. Even at that time, Rita shared my passion for empowering and inspiring others. Rita has now written a book, *Your Wow Years*, which guides people to thrive in their second half of life. I'm thrilled you've found this treasure.

As the founder and former CEO of Joie de Vivre Hospitality, I had the pleasure of meeting and working with many hotel salespeople. After having created and managed 50 boutique hotels (mostly in California) and sold my company, I enjoyed my subsequent time at Airbnb as Head of Global Hospitality and Strategy. I have pursued my passion for inspiring others through speaking, giving keynote talks, TED Talks and writing five books.

Rita's new book, *Your Wow Years*, seeks to help those over 50 to stay relevant in their careers and also addresses the broader spectrum of their lives. My book, *Wisdom at Work: The Making of a Modern Elder*, is part manifesto, part playbook, for people trying to stay relevant in the second half of their careers. Like *Modern Elder*, this particular book is important because paradigms in aging are changing with the shifting perceptions of "old and young". As you can see from her section on the new archetypes, "30 is no longer the prime of your life"; it is just the beginning! I encourage a new generational contract in the workplace in which everyone is valued, no matter their age. Rita's book expands upon this concept to include every aspect of your life.

Rita will help you supercharge your second half of life. You can actually improve your ability to create and live a "Wow Life" with age. We're fortunate that science has now proven that people are actually happier in their 50's and beyond. However, it doesn't just happen automatically by default. One needs to consistently practice a positive mindset, stay healthy and plan ahead. This is part of the reason I created a Modern Elder Academy in Baja California Sur (Mexico) to help people navigate midlife transitions and repurpose themselves with a new mindset.

I'm writing this foreword because initially Rita Connor and I shared a passion for the hospitality industry, knowing that travel gives people an enhanced experience of themselves. Little did I know that we would both be privileged to help "Modern Elders" stretch, explore and expand their next, most important chapter of life yet.

Chip Conley, Founder, Modern Elder Academy
San Francisco, California, 2019

Introduction:

Your Wow Years

"If you take care of the minutes,
the years will take care of themselves."

~ Tibetan saying

Why should you care about making your second half of life
your most awesome chapter ever? Because your biggest wow's in
life can be from the age of 50 onward. This is it. You can truly
supercharge the second half of your life, which I call your wow
years. I help you discover what lights you up, what you *really* want
to be doing in your second half of life, and create a plan—a blue-
print—then lean into and rock your next chapter, what I call Act
3, or even more powerfully—your wow years!

I have reinvented myself several times over the past 40 years.
I am a veteran of the corporate treadmill world and through my
passion for this subject, I became adept at reinventing myself and
teaching others how to do the same. If you're entering or living
in your second half of life, you start to realize it's now or never.
How can you create a wow day and ultimately a wow life?

Reasons

You may be in a job or a mundane life that you're just endur-
ing, asking if this is *it*? Is this all there is? How do you change
and get out of this rut? You must be willing today to grow and
change for these three important reasons:

1. You don't want the status quo, which is what you'll get if you keep doing what you're doing.
2. You can't avoid the inevitable fact that we're all going to die someday, and that day is closer than before. Are you going to limp along or finally take charge of your life?
3. Change helps you grow and offers opportunities with more choices; these have a ripple effect so you can create a much more fulfilling life.

This is a good time to reflect and ask yourself some important questions:

What makes your heart sing?
Do people know the real you?
What inspires you?
When do you lose track of time?
What would your soul *love* to do now?
What was your favorite or best age?

Guess what? It can be *now*! Your best time can be this next chapter of your life. Your biggest wows can actually be from 50 onward, and even if these questions appear to be stumbling blocks for you right now, I assure you by the end of the book, you will have the answers and solutions for how to create a wow life.

Are you disillusioned and weary of the life you've been living? I'll show you how to reinvent yourself and transition to live a much more passionate, fulfilled life—your wow years—sharing power tools I wish I'd known 10 or 20 years ago. Resilience—how to bounce back from life's setbacks and heartbreaks faster, where your lows are higher through subtle shifts. You'll learn how to tap into the high frequency of love—loving yourself a little bit more every day. You'll go from "I like me and I like who

I'm becoming" to "Wow, I love who I've become and who I'm *BEING!*" You'll discover how to get out of your way and co-create with God your future. You won't figure this all out tomorrow, but awareness is the start.

"When you do the conscious work, you don't age—you sage" (Zalman Schacter Sonomi).

I will help you uncover your passions and transition to your most awesome chapter of life ever. The theme most prominent in my life was, *I know I want something else—something more—but how do I get there?* I'll guide you through my process. It could actually be more fun to semi-retire. Why am I the person? What helped *me?* I overcame my fears by constantly trying new things; I've stumbled, fallen down, and learned how to bounce back. I attended countless seminars, read tons of self-help books, sought personal growth; did affirmations and passionately sought out powerful new methods to overcome adversity through personal growth, organizing retreats, learning to speak up, taking emotional risks, and then leading workshops. We're so fortunate to be living in this time of openness to spiritual and metaphysical principles. From the movie, *The Secret* to Dr. Deepak Chopra and Dr. Wayne Dyer's many books, Eckhart Tolle's writings to Dr. Bruce Lipton, and Dr. Joe Dispenza's books and videos on neuroscience and spirituality—there have never been more exciting, powerful opportunities for us to expand our consciousness.

My life has been a unique laboratory for learning to bounce back; studying and sharing tools to stay positive and high-vibe; constantly learning, stretching, growing, and sharing new ideas; doing something brave, bold, and new every day, through defining moments; facing my shadow self and staying in a high-vibe state.

I redesigned my perfect job every few years, planned my escape from the corporate world, creating my own successful company, Elite Resorts & Spas; then I reinvented myself, taught

Reinvent Yourself workshops, became a Licensed Professional Coach, and Certified Seminar Leader, ultimately finding my true calling and I am now fulfilling my destiny.

If you're over 50, you've already climbed a lot of mountains. When are you going to stand on top and enjoy the view? Will the *real you* please stand up? When do you feel most like yourself? Do you even know how that feels? Ever wonder how you can make sense of your life's twists and turns? How can you find your voice? You can reframe the adversity you've experienced and be proud you're now stronger in the broken places.

Through my journey of leaving my ex and the ranch of my dreams, overcoming my like-aholic tendencies, learning to speak up, owning my power, finding my voice after heartbreak, to discovering true happiness and fulfilling my dharma, I'll share tools that empower you, until you transition to the most awesome chapter of your life ever.

If you're a man or woman 50 years and over who has gained some life experience and are now ready for change—divorced, married, single, value exercise and health, optimistic, introverted, or extroverted—this book is for you.

Of all the ways I help clients, I get them out of the pain of *not* creating their wow lives. What you will sacrifice in not doing so is missing out on *joy* and fully realizing your true potential. Life becomes more precious as the years go on. You've had some important life experiences already and have gained wisdom. You don't want to die with your fondest dreams and deepest passions still inside you, waiting to come out.

I've added some of my workshop questions and processes as action steps at the end of each chapter so this book can complement and support my workshops and coaching services. It would be helpful to have a journal or your laptop handy to write your answers and thoughts after reading the action steps. If you're experiencing physical disease or emotional distress, it may feel challenging to reach your goals and aspirations. In working with people of all backgrounds, I've witnessed that these tools and techniques can be a powerful pathway to wellness.

Fully commit to making these your wow years. The most important moment in your life is this minute and the *next* one! What will you do to create more wow moments in your life? Read on and learn how to put more wow in your now!

Chapter One

Ready...Launch! Your Wow Years

You are more interesting now that you are older, with more life experiences to draw upon. Your thoughts are even more interesting! You have a broader frame of reference. When we have an aha in our mature years, it can be more exciting; it is richer and deeper in experience. Act 3, the years from 60-90 were formerly called golden years or the Indian summer of life. Who says your prime of life is in your thirties? I call *these years* the wow years because they have the potential to be the most dynamic, fun, surprising, enjoyable years ever; so full of awe, passion, and purpose. My wow years started in my fifties, and now in my sixties, my thoughts are more profound. I look at a sunset with more wonder. I listen to a song on the radio and muse about the singer, the melody, why they wrote those words, and I relate to the emotions of the song as a richer, deeper, more mature woman.

The wow-life/wow-day concepts are products of embracing all your knowledge. How did I come to the wow-now idea? Several years ago, I took a meditation class in Venice, California and the mantra the guru gave us to repeat during meditation was, "Present moment, wonderful moment."

"If that phrase is too long," he said, "You can just say 'Wow, now.'"

I loved that. All we have is the present moment. Wow, now! We don't have the past anymore and we don't have the future. The present moment is the only thing that's real. All we *ever* have is now. That became my new platform for helping likeminded people move into the best years of their lives. Mindfulness meditation is being in the present moment, accepting the present moment, being okay in the moment. Saying the mantra, "Wow, Now!" over and over makes the possibilities more exciting and you can feel happy with the present moment. With this Wow-now attitude, you'll bounce out of bed in the morning like an energizer bunny ready for the amazingly awesome day ahead!

Action step

Try the wow-now mantra this week in your meditation. Say, "Wow," breathing in for five counts. Hold for five counts, and then breathe out saying, "Now," for five counts.

How can we put some real wow into these years? It's true that finances and health are big factors, but why can't we make the last third of our lifetime, from 60-90 years old, our best chapter ever? One of my friends, Gigi who is 58 years old laughs and says, "My twenties and thirties were my bullshit years. Thank God, my hardest years are over!" This may not be true for all of us, but Gigi is now living her most rewarding and satisfying years ever. My friend, Adrian, says that in his thirties and forties he was always striving hard, trying to outperform himself to "get there." Now that he's in his seventies, he feels his biggest struggles are behind him; he's achieved a lot of goals, he feels wiser in part because of the mistakes he's made in the past, and he is now thoroughly enjoying the fruits of his labors. Besides focusing a lot on family and grandchildren, you still need a vibrant life of your own.

Even though our culture seems to revere youthful looking people, I wouldn't want to be 20 or 30 years old again. I am truly loving my sixties. Many people in their fifties and sixties still look fantastic, are healthier, have more to offer with prior experience, and are more viable than people in past generations. We need to acknowledge a new stage around retirement age *before* old age. Marc Freedman, Encore.org founder and author of *The Big Shift: Navigating the New Stage Beyond Midlife*, says, "We're facing a 30-year vacation that we don't want and can't really afford." He adds, "There's a sweet spot, an intersection between two dimensions of life. He calls these the Bonus Years; the convergence of mortality, longevity, and urgency."

We are redefining what it means to be the age we are. We are healthier overall than our parents were at this age and we're living longer. At 60, we could live another 30-plus years. My dad, who was a general practice physician, said his number-one piece of advice is to be proactive about your health and *stay out of the hospital*. How old do you feel inside? If you are sick, depressed, or ill, it may be difficult for you to honestly feel 22 or 28 years old; however, many people 60 and older feel like they are still in their thirties. I do!

My friend, Robert, quoted his father who lived to be 96 years old. "I wish I would have known at 65 that I would live to be 96. I would have started a new career. Son, you should have a business plan for your ages of 60-90. You can grow older and stronger instead of older and feeble." My friend, Tina, said her 85-year-old mother takes off for her volunteer job several days a week, saying, "I need to go work with my seniors now." In her mind, *she* is not a senior; she's just *volunteering* with the seniors.

As you enter the wow years, study up on healthy eating, exercise, well-being, and balance. You can actually grow older and better. Learn how to stay healthy and energetic because it's now more important than ever to ask what you really want out of life. When you hear the answers, I am going to help you to go for it. What do you have to lose?

The key to deciding what you want in your wow life is making a habit of listening to your soul, being brave, and honoring what comes to you. Thomas Moore, author of *Care of the Soul* suggests we ask what our soul would *love* to do today. The first time I ever bravely answered this question, it was a grey February day and I decided my soul really wanted to go to Barnes and Noble Bookstore and buy a Spa Finders magazine because I was interested in the new spa resorts that were opening up around our country.

I was a sales director of a luxury hotel chain at the time and I went against my self-disciplined, Catholic-girl upbringing of diligently making sales calls and prospecting new accounts. That day I'd just had it. I had been betrayed by my ex, unfairly lost a Windstar Cruise I had validly won for Best Salesperson of the Year, and I consequently felt no more loyalty for my current employment at a top luxury hotel chain. That day changed my life and I never looked back; I answered the question and followed my intuition. I bought the magazine, brought it home, and started calling all the spa resorts in the magazine, asking if they would be interested in hiring an independent contractor to promote group business to their resort. Sundance Resort was my first yes, then Ojai Valley Inn, then Royal Palms Resort, then five other resorts came on board, and this ultimately launched my new company, Elite Resorts & Spas. It was a game changer for me. Elite Resorts & Spas was a very successful enterprise for me for the last 18 years.

You never know what will happen when you ask and then honestly answer the question of what your soul would *love* to do today. It was life-changing because I changed an old habit and acted on my answer. My wow years really kicked in for me after that. It takes courage to follow up on what your soul would *love* to do.

Action step

Each morning, ask yourself what your soul would *love* to do today. Take time now to write it in your journal, meditate, and then write your answer.

You can continue to use this practice in every new act of your wow years. A couple years ago, I reinvented myself again and launched another act of my wow years, building my coaching business while continuing to run Elite Resorts & Spas. I was struggling between my usual self-discipline of getting my work done and longing to go out to play. The stirrings of spring fever tugged at me, saying, *Go outside, be in nature, take a deep breath, look up at the blue sky, get some fresh air, take a day-cation.*

I felt conflicted between answering the call for adventure and fun and yet honoring my sense of responsibility and work ethic. I kept thinking, *I work for myself. I have the flexibility of schedule Enough of this 9am-5pm work routine.* I hopped in my car with a different destination in mind. Many times in my life prior to my wow years, I didn't give myself permission to take a day off. I would drive to the office on the jam-packed 405 Freeway in Los Angeles and wistfully wish I could just keep heading north. Now, I intuitively knew how to ask myself that core wow-years question: "What would my soul *love* to do today?"

My soul told me to go North to Ojai, my favorite town near Santa Barbara. A change of geography gives you a fresh new outlook and brings surprising answers to life's questions. As soon as I turned onto Highway 33, winding into the tranquility of Ojai, the stress dissipated and I exhaled, feeling more relaxed off the beaten path. I noticed the 200-year-old oak trees lining Highway 33, listened to favorite tunes in the car, and thought, *Wow -life can be so sublime!* The soundtrack of fabulous music playing in my car, in this very spiritual, tranquil place set the tone for a perfect day to play hooky from work. I drove up the winding road to Meditation Mount, explored Ojai Valley and the surrounding Topatopa Mountains, and walked through its village-like center dotted with art galleries and new-age shops. Now *that* was a wow day! I was so energized by my day-cation in Ojai that I worked with extra enthusiasm the next day, booking some good business and accomplishing so much more. You *can* have a soul-enriching, beautiful getaway day *and* be productive. You're filling the well when the well has run dry or putting fuel in your gas tank.

Action step

Can you think of some similar wow moments or days in your life where you took a u-turn and it all worked out in your favor? Write down some of your wow moments or days and share on my Facebook page (www.facebook.com/Your-Wow-Years) or Instagram (www.instagram.com/yourwowyears/) why they were so special.

In our wow years, if we are young at heart, we act like a younger person. How is this accomplished? Close your eyes. Sink into a quiet state. Take a long, deep breath and ask yourself how old you *feel?* Allow an age to come up without judgment. No matter what age you really are, we don't see ourselves in the mirror as the age we truly are. If we feel old, then we *are* old. Wayne Dyer would say, "Never let an old person grow into your body." We feel the age of our *soul.*

I've heard 48-year-olds start a sentence with, "Well, now that I'm *old...*" Yikes! I tell them, "But you're not old—you're still young! Why do you think you're old?" To me, old is being in a rut; comfortably numb; stuck in a routine; when you stop trying new things. Old is when you've sort of given up. Old is repeating the same stories over and over and talking about your glory days in your twenties as if that was your hey-day. Old is when you say, "I'm too old for that new technology," even when it could open up your world in a new way and connect you with your loved ones in a much more seamless, time-efficient way like through Facebook, Instagram, texting, or email.

Action step

How old do you feel? Ask a friend or family member how old he or she feels? The answers may *surprise* you.

12

With your re-found youthful glow, it's time to find and live your passion. Give thanks for every day because time is more precious. You can take a course, go back to college, take an improv class, and realize it is ok. You'll always be an amateur at something. How can you now give your gifts and talents? One of my friends calls this time in her sixties the rinse cycle. She realizes she has more years behind her than ahead of her so she wants to make sure every day counts. Her days are more precious so she's cleaning old, negative beliefs, forgiving old hurts, releasing some bad habits, and starting fresh.

Part of finding your passion is exploring your bucket list. A bucket list is defined as "a list of things that one has not done before but wants to do before dying."

It's a number of experiences or achievements a person hopes to have or accomplish during his or her lifetime. You want to hopefully check this list off before you kick the bucket. I've always wanted to go hot air ballooning so that's on my bucket list. Your bucket list should include all the things you still want to do in life. This is a time in your life when your bucket list can actually become your to-do list.

Action step

What do you want out of life? Go for it; you have nothing to lose. Write your bucket list now.

"If you want a new outcome, you will have to break the habit of being yourself, and reinvent a new self" (Dr. Joe Dispenza).

You're reflecting on time lived and time left to live, thinking more deeply about the purpose beyond yourself, going from freedom from work to freedom to work and leaving a legacy; finding a way to offer services and yet still have a continued income: practical idealism. I, for one, intend to make the next 30 years my wow years. I intend to be a cutting-edge version of me, to step up my game, to be the best version of me *ever*, to stay healthy, in good shape, to stay positive and vibrant. What do I now want out of life? I'm going for it. What do I have to lose? It's time to find more of my passions.

In my Reinvent Yourself and Re-Imagine Your Life workshops and retreats, I help people go from midlife to living with more purpose, passion, and productivity. How about being a creative consultant part time and serving others part time? You can conceivably live 30 more years when you're 55-60 years old, and there's a real need for a school for the second half of life. Some call it your encore career or the second act for the greater good; integrating what you've worked at for years and using your experience of prior employment to bring about greater good.

In order to achieve maximum joy and productivity in your wow years, you must keep stretching yourself and create new neural connections in your brain. This phenomenon is known as neuroplasticity, which is the change in neural pathways and synapses that occurs due to certain factors like behavior, environment, or neural processes. The human brain has the amazing ability to reorganize itself by forming new connections between brain cells, or neurons.

To encourage neuroplasticity in my brain, I have recently committed to doing something bold, something brave, and something new every day.

"Courage is the power to let go of the familiar." (Raymond Lindquist).

Do Something *Bold, Brave, and New* Every Day

Something *bold*—taking some risks with a fearless, daring spirit. A friend of mine always wanted to act in the theater, so she responded to the something-bold challenge by joining a community theater group. I just watched her perform in her first play and she was an excellent actress. She never would have known this if she hadn't stuck her neck out and tried. To find your some-thing-bold, follow this direction:

Ask yourself what outside-of-the-box ideas will stretch you in some way today, where you're using more of your talents and your full potential.

How can you be bold and do your job differently today, and at the same time expand and tap into your desire to serve others; something that will ultimately give you more fulfillment and more money?

Meditate, then write down new, bold ideas that come to you.

"When you cannot make up your mind which of two evenly balanced courses of action you should take, choose the *bolder*" (William Joseph Slim).

My answer to these same questions came a few years ago. I wanted to create a high-vibe hospitality salon discussion evening, like the famous salons of Paris with Gertrude Stein and Jean Paul Sartre. I handpicked 10 interesting colleagues and invited them to a discussion evening with tea, wine, and snacks, and I saw this evening as already completed. I saw myself expressing the high-est divine outcome—facilitating a stimulating discussion with this select group of colleagues. I did a mental rehearsal and saw this as a new tool to develop mastery; I trusted and allowed in spiritual non-attachment that everything is *for* me. I then ex-pected the evening to go right. Not only was it divine, but these evenings are still going strong to this day. I have organized these popular discussion evenings with friends and business colleagues for five years and the idea has really taken off in Los Angeles, Orange County, and San Diego.

What about something *brave*? Every day, do one thing you're afraid to do. This really moves you forward. Something brave could be calling a client you were afraid to call. There was a client named Ruth who had been a tough cookie—a bit cold and unre-ceptive in the past, but I knew she had business for me. I called her (it was my fifth attempt) and it was this time that she was actually warm and receptive. She wanted to see me and she finally had business for me. They say the average sale is made on the fifth call. I realized I like myself best when I'm brave. Brave is defined as "showing mental or moral strength to face danger, fear, or difficulty; ready to face and endure danger or pain; showing courage."

To be brave, ask yourself these questions: How can I move further out of my comfort zone today? What would life be like if I was more unlimited? What if I spoke up more courageously for what I want or to resolve conflict? A friend wanted to speak to me about a misunderstanding we had and I feared the conversation would involve risk and pain in hearing possible criticism about my actions; I felt brave as I called her. I took a deep breath and asked for courage to learn and grow from the conversation. It was painful at first, but we resolved the conflict. If I'm wanting to attract my soulmate, what if I bravely give men more clues I'm interested in them? Ninety percent of men who ask women out say the women showed interest in them first. One of my friends in her sixties, Jane won a dinner for two at a high-end restaurant and she bravely asked a friendly guy who walked his dog regularly in her neighborhood to join her. He eagerly accepted her invitation. A year and ten months later, they were married!

"Do one thing every day that scares you" (Eleanor Roosevelt). Anias Nin said, "And the day came when the risk to remain tight in a bud was more painful than the risk it took to blossom."

What about something *new*? A new pilates or yoga class, trying a new hairstyle, combining different clothes and jewelry to create a new outfit, trying a new spot for happy hour with friends or trying a new, healthy recipe that day all count in this category. The desire to try something new gives us the juice that keeps us learning, growing, and continuously expanding. Sometimes it feels like walking through mud to make that first step to something new. Deep-breathing exercises help me through this period. I'll say to myself, *Yikes, this is hard! But I can do this!* Change can be messy at times, but I'm not here to remain the same. I take a few deep breaths, and somehow, I slosh through the muck to the other side.

It's amazing how this promise to myself is moving me forward with so much speed in almost magical ways. I have a sticky note on my computer that reminds me to do something *bold, brave* and *new* today, and I won't let the day go by until I've done all three things.

Having someone to be accountable to when you are becoming brave and bold is important for success. My sister, Jackie and I played a game where we emailed each other our bold, brave, new actions we did each day. The new actions don't have to be too crazy. It's about thinking outside the box or doing something—anything—out of the norm at all for the typical day. "I went to a new place for coffee," could be enough. We have wavering strength so some days it could be simply, "I took a new route to work," while other days can be, "I set up a new workshop, got a beauty makeover, and signed up for a new class."

There will always be challenges. Get started now. With each attempt at something bold, you'll become stronger and more confident. It just may lead to the next big thing. How about it? Isn't the time ripe for a bold, brave, new *you*?

"If we're growing, we're always going to be out of our comfort zones" (John Maxwell).

Action step

Find an accountability partner and each commit to doing something bold, brave, and new every day. Email each other regularly about what you've done that is bold, brave, and new.

What can you do today that's bold, brave, and new? Write down some ideas in your journal.

Now we have a foundation set in place to build on to understand and create what you want in your wow years. You are ready to do the next phase of your work—understand what could come along to hold you back.

Chapter Two

What Holds Us Back From Our Wows

Old programs. Being self-conscious about our flaws. Limiting beliefs. Laziness. Unworthiness. Inadequacy. Fear of rejection. Fear of failure. Uncertainty. Loneliness. Change. Loss of freedom, etc. I am very supportive of personal development work. Like many Los Angeleno's, I have touched all sorts of corners and places of self-help and recovery. A woman from Chicago once said kiddingly to me, "Oh you're from La-La Land, the land of fruits and nuts". A wonderful aspect of life in LA is that a large group of my friends are on a continuous, enthusiastic personal development path. Acknowledging where you have come from is helpful to know how to approach where you are headed, but what are you going to do for the next twenty to thirty years? We have to release the past and move forward to do what we came here to do. It's now or never. This time in your life *can* be your wow years. What would you like to accomplish in the next two or three decades so that they truly are your wow years?

One of the first ways to engage your wow years is to take a look at your current biggest challenge or block. Believe it or not, it is actually perfect for you. You can reframe the challenge with this question: How is what I am going through perfect for what I came here to do? Let me show you how to understand the connection to your path of life *despite* what is happening to you.

What are fueling your biggest challenge are your biggest flaws; however, what if your flaws could be your biggest assets?

"How is what you're going through actually perfect for what you came here to do? What if your flaws were actually part of your perfection? What if your flaws could actually be your gift?" (Mastin Kipp).

What if you lived your life without having a mother's love? What if your mother told you that you would never achieve anything? What if she kept calling you wild and uncontrollable? My 56-year-old friend, Jennifer was raised by a mother who tried to pummel the wildness out of her at a very young age, with physical beatings and verbal abuse. Jennifer embraced her inner voice, for in her mind, her ability to be untamed by her mother meant freedom. When Jennifer finished college and had to move home for a short time, her mother threw out all her belongings onto the front lawn because she could not pay rent. She spent years focused on making money with the motivation that she would never have to return and live in a home without love. In 2009, she started her volunteer work to help end human trafficking. She actually labeled this period of her life fighting to live.

Jennifer believed her biggest flaw was that she was not listening to her higher guidance. In 2018, Jennifer spent time journaling and working through Rick Warren's, *The Purpose-Driven Life* and she could finally hear the voice in the wilderness. She realized her childhood experiences could help free other children and they too could fight to live. She also finally realized that *love* is the answer; we must lay our own lives down for another. No matter the socio-economic level, we are connected with the need to love our neighbors. In her case, Jennifer believes God also gave her the name Wild with a different meaning. She has been placed on this earth to help set others free. She calls this time in her life "luv'in freedom" and she believes she is God's wild child. She is inspired by Jewel's song, *Hands*: "I won't be made useless;

I won't be idle with despair; I will gather myself around my faith."

The major flaw in my character was *not speaking up*. While growing up, I was taught by my proper English mother to be very polite. While I appreciate that she and my Canadian dad taught their children to be self-effacing, respectful, well-mannered, and diplomatic, I took this need to please and be polite to the extreme. My mother said the best hostess is the one who shows an interest in other people, never talks about religion, money, or politics, and makes everyone feel good about themselves—make them feel like the evening just wouldn't have been the same without them there. I was always able to make friends easily, but it has consistently been a challenge for me to bring up issues that might cause distress or a conflict with people, even when I needed to speak up. I've shied away from fights, violence, arguments, altercations, and clashes.

I had to ultimately take public speaking classes and join Toastmasters to find my voice, because of this conditioning in my childhood. A voice inside me finally screamed, *Will the real Rita* please *stand up and speak up?*

Life isn't always smooth, and when something is morally wrong, it takes courage to fight bravely for a cause. I admire people who unabashedly argue or oppose something that's unfair or unjust, who fight something unpleasant, prevent or stop wrong doing. It's a fine line; I learned a tough lesson the hard way recently that being polite and pretending everything is ok on the surface in order to avoid conflict takes its toll. In order to move forward to embrace and take on your wow years' dreams and goals, you need to be able to speak up. You don't want to continue to be a like-aholic like I was (a concept I will explain in more detail in a later chapter).

Eventually, if you don't talk about important issues, they find a way of bubbling to the surface and exploding. You can inadvertently orchestrate an end to a relationship by default. Two of my friendships ended because, for too long, I avoided expressing my own feelings of anger and other deep concerns that needed to be discussed and hashed out. I've been thinking that possibly these friendships could have been preserved if we had ventured to talk to each other honestly, with courage, compassion, love, and mutual respect. It's important to have clear boundaries and communicate in a loving, diplomatic way in order to sustain friendships in our wow years. The challenge with one of the friendships was that my friend lived eight hours away and he hated the phone, preferring texts and emails. Misunderstanding resulted from both of us reading between the lines. Texting isn't really the best form of communication when you're having a disagreement.

It was finally time for the real Rita to please stand up. After losing those two friends, I recently had a similar situation come up again, but this time I spoke up. I risked telling the truth and losing the person. I figured, *well, I will lose them anyway because it can't go on like this anymore.* I expressed myself through a phone call since I couldn't do it in person. I fought for my principles but wasn't impolite. I was gracious and diplomatic. I realized I like myself so much better when I'm brave. We talked the whole situation out using the conflict resolution process below and we actually became closer friends afterward. Telling the truth, I risked hurting the other person and yes—Ouch!—sometimes it can hurt on both sides, but it's more painful in the long run to keep stuffing your feelings and not being authentic.

Action step

Conflict resolution does not have to involve sparks and a big fight. Here's a great technique I learned that's helpful if you're having a disagreement or misunderstanding with someone. This conflict-resolution process helps diffuse defensiveness and lets both people participate in fixing the problem. It's very powerful.

First, set up a time or an appointment to talk to the person you are having a conflict with. Ask, "When would be a convenient time for us to talk about a few things?"

At that time, say to the person you are having the conflict with: "_____ (their name), what I appreciate about our relationship is that... (Here are some examples: we have always been honest with each other, you've always been fair with me, we've always been supportive of each other, we've always tried to help each other, etc.)"

Next, say, "What I'm having a challenge with right now is..." or, "What concerns me lately is..." or, "I felt (confused or hurt) about..." then state your problem to them.

Third, say, "What would work a little better for me would be if you could possibly..." (make a suggestion here), or, "What would be helpful to me is if you could possibly..." or, "What I would like to do is..." or, "What I need from you is..."

Fourth, ask, "What do *you* think we could do to make this more of a win-win situation? What suggestions do you have to make this work a little better for both of us?"

Another setback I had to grapple with was a physical byproduct of anxiety. I experienced a frightening condition on a stressful day involving a huge lump in my throat. I first encountered this odd ailment after I had split up with my ex and was buying a new house on my own for the first time. Workmen were busy remodeling my new home, I was moving into a home office, I had a stressful job, and to top it off, some clients were upset and frustrated with me. I was discouraged, overwhelmed, and stressed out. Can you identify with that? I was on complete overload! I had paperwork piled high and my personal life seemed to magnify all my challenges. It was 5:30pm, I was caught in rush hour traffic in Manhattan Beach— five jam packed lanes on both sides of the road—smelling the traffic exhaust. I could hear my own breath, which got shorter and shorter and shorter to the point where I couldn't breathe. *Yikes! Is this what they call a Panic Attack?* I couldn't swallow and I thought, *Oh, my God! I'm going to have to get out of my car in this bumper-to-bumper traffic, shake this off, and do some deep-breathing techniques.* The people-pleaser inside me was worried the guy behind me might get angry that I had to get out of my car. This aggravated the condition more. I kept saying, "Mind over matter," over and over and managed to pull over to the side of the road after the light changed. Later, I heard two words from my doctor that I'd never heard before. The doctor said I had Globus Hystericus. It is an anxiety-induced state and your throat closes up due to stress. There's a lump in the throat so big you can't breathe or swallow.

I learned mindfulness meditation techniques to handle the stress as a result and it made a positive lasting impact on helping me. One was this Kaiser Permanente recommended technique: Breathe in for five counts, hold for five counts, and out for five counts. I learned what doesn't kill us makes us stronger. Stress caused all these things and mindfulness was the solution. The gift of overcoming this adversity of anxiety was learning mindfulness breathing techniques that I still use to this day, and I was forced to slow down. I had adrenal fatigue and could no longer run on empty like I had before. My creativity was being thwarted and my body was sending me overt signals.

Action step

I'm sure you have had big challenges that at the time were pretty stressful but you learned something constructive from them. Write about a life challenge that brought you to a new lesson or learning either at work or at home. How did you bounce back on a bad day and turn this into a win or a success?

How else can we get a handle the fears and limiting beliefs that hold us back from our wow life? Take note of your current state of mind. Fears can dissipate if they are balanced with hope and optimism. I make a list called "What is the greatest?"

Here is my list:

- Greatest fear—fear (Fear of fear causes more problems in our lives than fear itself.)
- Greatest day—today
- Greatest mistake—giving up
- Greatest stumbling block—ego
- Easiest thing to do—find fault
- Greatest comfort—work well done
- Greatest need—common sense
- Greatest gift—forgiveness

Many people avoid doctor's appointments, parties, asking for a raise, or trying new things due to the memory of a fear. Ask yourself how this moment would be without the fear. I love to say, "Fear is a friend I take with me on all my new adventures."

What would your experience be like without the fear of failure? Have you ever thought the moment could be an adventure rather than a fearful failure? It would be exciting and purely *fun*. I could treasure this incredible moment after all; it's the culmination of all the other moments of my life. How?

I'll explain. The universe is **for** us. I could write for days on the subject of vibration and frequency and empowerment tools to diminish the past conditioning and help you no longer be held back. I love practicing new techniques and having aha's. I've learned we're wired for joy and life *is* rigged in our favor. Yes, the universe is *for* us.

"Every thought or feeling has a vibration that can be measured. When you raise these vibrations, you connect to the power of intention. That place is the sweet spot where you feel joy, happiness, and your dream life becomes your reality." (Wayne Dyer).

It's fascinating that being and living in a high-vibrational, high-frequency state is where it's at. That's where all the good stuff happens. Gregg Braden in *Walking Between the Worlds* said when we are in *fear*, this is how our DNA's double helix looks:

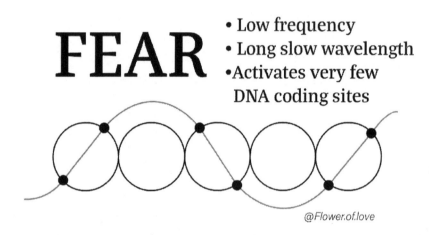

FEAR
- Low frequency
- Long slow wavelength
- Activates very few DNA coding sites

@Flower.of.love

There are fewer coding points for our amino acids and enzymes to flow through. It's like a valve is pinched closed. There's a kink in our hose and life just doesn't flow.

When we're feeling love in a joyful, high-vibe state, this is how the double helix looks. Excited, enthusiastic, joyful, loving feelings are flowing through us. There are more coding points connecting. We are truly wired for joy. Energy flows through the hose and life *flows*. It's so exciting!

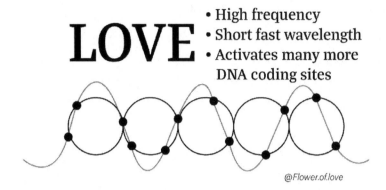

LOVE
- High frequency
- Short fast wavelength
- Activates many more DNA coding sites

@Flower.of.love

Joy, passion, enthusiasm, love, gratitude, positive feelings, and excitement are at the top of the vibrational scale, so how do we vibrate at a higher frequency?

For starters, you can act *as if* you're at a higher vibration. If you live this way, you have less need to bounce back because you are already in an open, receptive state and channeling less negativity. We can change little things until we get a big wow moment, and then our life suddenly starts to vibrate at a higher frequency. We are like a singing bowl; change little things and our life suddenly takes off. Time to fire on all cylinders; bing, bing, bing.

To help raise my frequency, I created a list of my high-vibe to-do's:

- Read books and attend seminars that stretch me
- Listen to Wayne Dyer and other stimulating thought leaders
- Listen to more TED talks
- Write my own TED Talk
- Stretch my body through pilates and get more cardio
- Eat more organic fruits and veggies
- Take more hikes in nature and try new trails

- Get up 30 minutes earlier and meditate every day
- Forgive more quickly and have more compassion
- Become a more conscious listener
- Listen with reverent alertness
- Be willing and open to change my opinion
- Be less self-righteous
- Become more vulnerable
- The list goes on and on...

Below is a vibrational scale that goes from 1-10. At the top of the scale (10) are the qualities of love, joy, passion, and empowerment. At the very bottom of the scale is grief, depression, hopelessness, and despair. Imagine you're vibrating at a seven and you want to be vibrating at a nine or 10. Ask yourself what you will do when you're at a 10. How will you feel? It sounds simple, but you'd do things that make you happy. It will build and build.

We have talked about getting into a positive frame of mind, a high-vibrational state, but how do you *stay* in that high-frequency state in your wow years when it's a grey November day, someone hangs up on you, you stub your toe, and spill coffee on your best shirt? We all have those days. How do you bounce back after those hiccups, speed bumps, and roadblocks? More people are working from their homes in virtual offices these days. How do you stay in that high-vibe state?

I've included the positive frame of mind chart above that shows the emotions ranging at the bottom of the scale from number one—grief, depression, hopelessness, despair—up to number 10, which is joy, highest excitement, empowerment, love, freedom, appreciation, and passion. Scientists have found that we are actually wired for joy. Have you ever noticed that

A Positive Frame of Mind Every Day
Aim for the 8-10 "Sweet Spot!"

10	Joy - Highest Excitement - Empowerment - Love – Freedom – Appreciation - Passion
9	Happiness - Gratitude - Compassion - Courage
8	Inspired - Confidence - Responsible - Open-Hearted - Serene
7	Empowered - Worthy - Eagerness - At Ease - Light-Hearted
6	Hopefulness - Encouraged - Acceptance - Faith - Positive
	Neutrality - Quiet Center of Stillness
5	Doubtful - Insecurity - Lonely - Rejection - Disappointment
4	Worry - Pessimism - Frustration - Impatience - Irritation
3	Anger - Rage - Revenge - Hatred - Fear
2	Sadness - Abandoned - Ashamed - Anxiety - Unloved
1	Grief - Depression - Hopelessness - Despair

Abraham-Hicks Vibrational Emotional Scale

when you're feeling happy, loving, enthusiastic, grateful, and you're in a good mood, more good actually comes into your life? The good stuff happens when you're in that 8-10 sweet spot feeling optimism to enthusiasm. But how do you stay in the 8-10 sweet spot of the chart? You can see how we're wired for joy when you refer back to the diagram of the DNA's double helix discussed and posted earlier. Where do you register now on this scale? When we're feeling **fear**, we actually pinch off our valve, like there's a kink in your hose, so to speak. Our double helix contracts and there are fewer coding points for our amino acids and enzymes to connect and flow energy. On the other hand, when we're flowing **loving** energy, the double helix expands and our amino acids and enzymes have more coding points to connect, so we actually flow energy to what we want. I've listed action steps to raise your vibration: how to Pivot, Rebound, Course-correct, and Reinvent yourself.

1. Take three *deep* belly breaths.
2. Meditate: connect to higher self—divine source
3. Ask what's bothering you
4. Write: "Dump the chatter" in your journal
5. Ask what your soul would *love* to do today. How can you serve others today? What brings you JOY?
6. Do that, be that, share that, and get more joy
7. Be grateful: say thank you, thank you, thank you
8. Affirmation: "I expand in love, success, and abundance every day as I inspire those around me to do the same."
9. Say intentions, pre-pave your day in segments.
10. Get fresh air. Go outside into *nature*
11. Exercise: move your body, get a massage
12. Practice power poses before meetings and appointments
13. Drink lots of water. Eat more plant-based foods and less sugar.
14. Listen to your favorite upbeat music
15. Look at your vision board or dream book often
16. Schedule activities with positive, high-vibe friends
17. Laugh/sing/dance at least once a day
18. Take action: *brave*, new steps that move you forward
19. Visualize whenever you can
20. Mantra for those challenging days: "I have no idea how, but somehow this is going to work out to my ultimate

advantage. It's going to be fun to see how the universe works this situation out for me. Something *good* is happening to me because of this!"

21. Intend to vibrate in the sweet spot between 8-10
22. Plan and expect things to *go right*

Action step

Write 25 high-vibe to-do's you'll be doing when you're at a 10. What books will you be reading? What high-vibe superfoods will you be eating? What new positive behaviors will you have; will you be taking more walks, maybe playing an instrument? Taking some classes? Write down mental, physical, spiritual, emotional things you'll do. When you're doing them, act *as if* you're at a higher vibration.

If you take these simple steps, you'll feel a greater sense of wholeness and completion.

People with the same sense of wholeness will be attracted to you. You'll attract your equal. It truly is the law of attraction we've heard so much about.

Being in a higher-vibrational positive state can change our reality. Quantum science is now proving through major experiments that we are all connected. We truly are part of a matrix. Once we understand our connection to the universe, we can recognize the powerful strength of our thoughts.

"When we realize that every atom we are made of has an infinite connectivity to all things, then we start to feel our role in the larger picture" (Nassim Huramein).

According to Rupert Sheldrake, ideas can actually spread around the world in the morphogenetic field through the collective unconscious. We are so fortunate to now be able to access many YouTube videos that show how our emotions affect our DNA. Author/Speaker, Gregg Braden has some of the best videos on this subject. Our emotions and beliefs and those we have inherited affect our DNA. Our genes respond to emotions for better or worse. Studies show that the mind and body are not separate. "The very molecules in our bodies are responsive to our psychological environment. Stress and emotions affect our DNA. The winding of the DNA helix is associated with DNA repair and the unwinding precedes all cell division. Focused, loving feelings and specific intentions alter the DNA." (Gregg Braden)

The universe leaves us love notes. Love notes from the universe are signs along the way. Watch for those signs. When you ask for a sign, be alert and watch for the answers. The answers could come through messages on billboards, bumper stickers, or chance phone calls. God-winks are happening all the time if you're watching for them and take notice. The universe leaves breadcrumbs like Gretel in the fairytale, but when you're on the wrong frequency, you walk right past them. Life is magical. Continuously release the fear and your consciousness will continue to expand. Gratitude changes your physiology and it can actually open locked-up blessings.

Say, "Thank you, thank you, thank you." This raises your vibration. Then pump your fist and say, "Universe, bring it!"

You can see that old, repetitive, disempowering programs can hold you back from having a wow. Before you can fully align with your new goals, it's time to dig a little deeper to uncover everything that could hold you back. When people unconsciously emulate their parents, we've heard the saying, "He comes by it honestly," or "the apple doesn't fall far from the tree." Yes, we inherit a lot from our parents, including their positive traits and often well-meaning, yet bad examples.

Chapter Three
Will I Ever Be Enough?

Joni is a very popular, successful yoga teacher in Los Angeles with a loyal following. At this point in her life, she realized there always seemed to be some kind of ailment torturing her throughout her entire life. In her early years, she suffered with food issues and crazy eating patterns, then an ankle problem that interfered with her dancing career, then facial eczema that was debilitating during her modeling career, then sciatica and shoulder pain trying to derail her yoga career. The list went on and on, always some malady to take her attention away from the joy, momentum, and *responsibilities* of her life, which is the core issue about ailments—not wanting to grow up and be responsible.

Finally, Joni is identifying and realizing that this need to focus on the body non-stop is the result of suppressing her emotions, a trait she picked up from her mother and ancestry. Her mom was an extremely kind, caring, and giving person, but she had non-stop ailments throughout her life that became very serious in her later years. Her mother would actually say: "I got sick to get attention." It is possible this was also a result of her need to repress negative emotions and continue appearing to be good, perfect, and loving to all. Joni has been waking up, identifying this inherited trait, and doing inspirational reading, yoga, meditation, mindfulness, prayer, and other treatment modalities to understand and heal this forever.

As you make new decisions for how to spend your wow years, you may not have looked closely at inherited traits—qualities from our ancestors. It's never too late to learn more about our inherited traits, as they can work against us or in our favor. We make the choice how to process what we discover about our past and apply it into our current lives. We inherit genetic memory—memories "present at birth that exist in the absence of sensory experience" (Collins Dictionary). It is incorporated into the genome over long spans of time. It is based on the idea that common experiences of a species become incorporated into its genetic code. My parents both passed away at the advanced ages of 86 and 92 in 2008. I just recently started to sort through the final two storage bins behind my garage that hold their special photos, letters, and mementoes—items I just couldn't throw away.

I found an old suitcase in one of the bins belonging to my grandmother, Ida O'Connor, who lived in Winnipeg, Manitoba, Canada. The suitcase hadn't been opened since my dad received it after his mother's funeral in 1978, and its locks were old and rusted. Secrets wafted out of the old, dusty suitcase and they called out to me to be uncovered. A musty energy washed over me as I lifted out letters, diaries, and trinkets from the past. I found a delicate, white christening gown worn by my father as a baby in 1917—now 100 years ago.

There were letters and many black-and-white photos from the Connor family of Canada. I found a special, old photo of my handsome grandfather, Jack B. Connor. I noticed a sadness and pain in his eyes. I lifted from an envelope photos of my dad's sister, Jean, who, at 15, on a frozen lake in Manitoba fell through the ice with the family dog and tragically drowned. I teared up a bit thinking of death and that light dimming. My dad always had a fear of drowning stemming from this incident. Sad that I never had the chance to even meet Grandpa Connor, who died working in the Saskatchewan oil fields in the far-off west when my father was 10 years old.

As I went through the old diplomas, awards, medals, and letters, I thought of how our ancestors pass on a lot more than their genes or DNA. I saw the discipline of my dad's studies, a 10-year-old riding his bike on a paper route to help support his mother and brother when his father died. He was eager to learn and very self-motivated, as he spent hours at the Swan River Library. My dad taught the Cree Indians of Manitoba and was very compassionate to their plight on the reservation. He eventually became a successful physician and surgeon, teaching us kindness, curiosity, love of fellow man, generosity, and compassion for the underdog. He had a huge heart and passion for learning and self-improvement. These qualities are his lasting legacy that never dies.

Looking at the photos, I felt like I time travelled back into their lives. It's important to review your family's past and decide what it means to you. What I learned on that afternoon journey down memory lane was that my relatives passed on lasting lessons in dignity, generosity, faith in God, and charity through much joy and pain. Both my parents had an outstanding way of sharing with us humor, wisdom, culture, values, and knowledge. I was blessed to inherit a lot of positive traits along with the negative.

We also inherit genetic pain as part of our genetic memory. If there was discord or trauma, you could have brought that legacy into your own life, and it could contribute to what holds you back in your current life. This might sound a bit out there, but I have seen people go through alternative therapeutic methods to discard inherited traits and I've actually witnessed the difference.

I knew a Jewish girl named Amy. Every time she was happy, she felt guilty because she would think of her sad grandmother and great grandmother who lost everything in Stalin's Russia. She wanted to be a dancer and she felt so much joy in dance. I participated in her Family Constellation Therapy in Santa Monica. This young woman played herself, the therapist recreated the great grandmother's village, one person played the part of Stalin, others played her grandparents, aunts, uncles, and the villagers. That evening, we helped her heal the traumatic, painful, genetic memory inflicted by Stalin's Russia. Why are we who we are? Sometimes people like Amy inherit survivor guilt.

"Memories pass between generations. Behavior can be affected by events in previous generations, which have been passed on through a form of genetic memory, animal studies suggest. Experiments showed that a traumatic event could affect the DNA in sperm and alter the brains and behavior of subsequent generations" (BBC News).

Most of us still hear our mother's or father's voices in our heads. They shaped a vision for us that's not really our own. My mother was a bit of an English snob and throughout my life I felt like I was always having to stick up for America. Lately, I've been pondering about the tendency people have to think they're better than whatever race, nationality, or culture they have deemed inferior. This is an opportune time in your life to shine a light on inherited prejudices, let them go, and embrace a more tolerant, enlightened point of view. I also often hear my father's voice. Whenever I praise myself too much, I can still hear him saying, "Now, now, Rita. No one likes a bragger."

The Lakota have a saying, "Aho Mitakuye Oyasin" which means to honor all my relations—everyone who came before me, and everyone who will come after me. By looking at your past, you are honoring how you got to where you are today. While there can be pain in looking back, especially if there is a history of abuse or alcoholism, you could be discounting any good. There is a generation coming up after you, and the work you do on your ancestors will also set them free to create new behavior and patterns. *TOOTS + MARY*

Action step

Do you have some old family photos stored in your garage or attic? Have a look at them and see if you get a deeper insight into who you really are. What family traits, prejudices, vices, or special qualities did you inherit from your ancestors? Which are you most grateful for? Is it time to release some of their inherited, negative traits?

We can also be held back by our formative impressions of ourselves. I was born in Winnipeg, Manitoba, Canada and was raised in Playa del Rey, California in a big Irish Catholic family with three brothers and four sisters. It was a happy childhood full of lots of love and laughter, but from the ages of nine to 14 years old, I was not very cute. My older sister was a gorgeous model with John Robert Powers Modeling School and I was a late bloomer who felt I always had to try harder. I got voted most talented in eighth grade due to my art and musical talent; however, I had mousy hair, crooked front teeth, cat glasses, and just didn't feel pretty when I was younger. This feeling of low self-esteem carried through into young adulthood. I finally got braces on my teeth and started to bloom in my twenties. In my late twenties, people would actually introduce me saying, "This is Rita, my prettiest friend." I'd roll my eyes because I never believed them. Old beliefs die hard.

"What you are now is where you were when" is a theory from Morris Massey that helps us understand who we are and who we've become. The theory is that the "when" is around the time we reach those wonderful early teen years, age 14 or 15. Up until this age, the world is all about just ourselves. Now, we see ourselves as part of the world, we socialize, and we often start developing our outlook on life.

My engrained teen self-image stayed with me a long time.

I never felt beautiful no matter what compliments I would get, and always went the extra mile to try harder, work harder, and hoped maybe someday I'd be enough, but when do you *ever* know you're enough?

Action step

Do you ever say to yourself, *When will I ever be enough?* I felt I was always trying to be smarter, more successful, prettier, slimmer, etc. until I was just exhausted. One day after a lot of soul searching, I was hiking in the Santa Monica Mountains and I exhaled and shouted, "Wow! I am enough. I am more than enough!" What are your thoughts? Are you enough?

Another version of not good enough was my other subconscious mantra for many years, *When will my soul ever get it right?* I had to shake that off and found just doing something, *anything,* being brave, making a move, or trying something new, would help adjust my mindset. I tend to think we've lived many lifetimes and I'm sure this is the best *me* I've ever been. Is this the best version of *you* you've ever been?

In our everyday lives, we are constantly getting opportunities for growth by understanding that indiscretions triggering old, past wounds of unworthiness are opportunities for a mindset shift. Recently, I was very hurt by a male friend when he cancelled out at the last minute for a concert I'd been anxiously anticipating. I have always had a hot button about people who don't honor their commitments and cancel at the last minute with a lame excuse. He really hurt my feelings; I had already bought the tickets and when he cancelled by text saying "I can't go to the concert. So sorry I bailed on you," I actually felt a sharp, physical pain inside. It's interesting how emotional pain can actually cause a burning sensation inside our body. It's like his thoughtless action pierced my heart.

I took a deep breath and kept saying, "Something good is happening to me because of this," over and over, like a mantra. I knew on some level we must not be aligned energetically, but the focus was on how I was going to process this experience. I then said, "It's going to be fun to see how the universe works this out in my favor. All is well. Everything is working out for our highest good." I took another deep breath and chose to not take it personally. I could have pouted and ranted for days about how selfish and unfair he was, but in a way, I just didn't want to take it personally, dwell on it, and drink the poison. I knew it was best to focus on confidence that his actions don't bother me. I'll be too busy to care. I'm just going to say, "Next!" Guess what?! I met a wonderful new guy that following week and invited him to the concert instead. Thank God this other guy had bailed and created the space for someone *so* much better for me. Wow! It was divine timing.

We can bounce back, become stronger, and turn things around after suffering a disappointment or loss. They say, "Pain cracks you open so the light can get in." You can transform the pain and become what Carl Jung calls the wounded healer. It is never too late to allow this to happen in your life. Pain can force us to dig a deeper well, but we can actually fill that well with more compassion. When you face the pain of your own or of your parents' and loved ones' paths, you can help others through what you went through because having experienced and grown through the pain, you now have wisdom and credibility. As you seek to help others, you are in turn helping yourself. Your work serving others ultimately heals you too.

"The wound is where the light enters" (Rumi).

My friend, Anne, had a similar disappointment a few days later and I was able to share my story and help her because of what I just went through. I even had some great affirmations and tips to share with her. I felt more compassion for her situation.

Pain cracked me open and opened my heart to help a good friend, and it ultimately helped me create the space for someone so much better.

Action step

How can you take a disappointment or loss and become a wounded healer? How can you crack your heart open, help others, and ultimately help yourself?

We have had a life of hellos and goodbyes. Each of these relationships have been defining moments in our lives, and how we cope with them affects how we are held back from our wow years. We often hold onto relationships that can hold us back because it is too painful to see that we may find stronger connections with others. These choices are hard to make. I understand; I had to leave the first love of my life when the relationship no longer served me. I got my college degree, traveled to Europe, worked in London for a year, and dated several guys in my twenties. I started my career in sales for the hotel industry with Hyatt, Hilton, and Meridien Hotels. When I met Jim at the age of 29, he was charming, funny, successful, and daring. We were both at the same place in our lives. He and I had both dreamed of having a ranch with horses. We moved in together, fixed up five houses, and ended up in a beautiful home overlooking the Pacific Ocean in the hills of Malibu. He had two kids and we had nine animals. We learned a lot together, but after 10 years together, something just wasn't right.

I read the book, *Feel the Fear and Do It Anyway* by Susan Jeffers, which had an impact on me. She says, "Do what you fear, and the death of that fear is certain." It will increase your self-esteem. I wrote down, "What do I fear? Leaving Jim, getting a new job, doing public speaking," so I did all three.

It wasn't easy to leave him. It had been a ten-year investment that ended in his infidelity when I was 40. He was my world. I feared leaving him because I loved him and had lived the life of my dreams in idyllic Malibu, with two St. Bernard dogs and several cats, overlooking Zuma Beach. I woke up at 3:30am and knew in my heart I had to leave. He just wasn't the right guy. I knew he wasn't true to me on the business trips he took. I wasn't listening to myself, but I would think over and over, "I have to leave." One night, I had a nightmare about him and there were ugly ghouls dancing on our roof and all around our house. The next day in the kitchen, I overheard him say something to my sister that indicated to me that he really didn't honor and cherish me. I just knew that was it; time to leave. The defining moment of saying goodbye was before me, and I had to make the choice for Rita to take a new life path, even though it was a terrifying empty canvas.

I moved to Manhattan Beach. It was 1990, the AIDS epidemic had just kicked in, and I was so afraid to start dating again. In the middle of watching the musical *Evita* with Sarah Brightman singing "Don't Cry for Me Argentina," I had shortness of breath and couldn't breathe. I had just found out Jim had a new girlfriend and I knew it was really over. I was having a panic attack, so I got up and went through a row of 15 very annoyed people, during the highlight song of the evening, to try to breathe again and get some water out in the lobby. My world and everything that had been holding me up was dissipating, crumbling, and disappearing. I had read about Cher and Jane Fonda's moments of clarity when they left their spouses and I knew I had been correct about embracing my defining moment of leaving him, although at this moment it felt awful.

It was the final straw. I had always put him on a pedestal, like my mom put my dad on a pedestal. I learned the hard way that no one should ever be on a pedestal. We all need to be eye to eye. I had rented a little house in Manhattan Beach and at night I'd open the gate and stare at the front door so forlorn and afraid to go into that dark little house. This was the first time in my life I had ever lived alone.

Action step

List defining moments where you showed up in a brave, new way, stood up for yourself, and overcame some big fears. Did you feel like a different person afterwards?

What about other defining moments you have ignored and let pass?

I never even said goodbye to Jim's two children, who were 13 and 10 years old, when I left. He moved in with another woman right after I moved out. I walked away from the children without that closure because I didn't feel like they valued me or even cared to say goodbye to me. That was my assumption, not their words, from my old conditioning. I was also trying to protect myself so I wouldn't hear about him and the other woman. I know I didn't waste the ten years because I truly loved Jim and his children. I learned a lot, experienced some really happy times together, and we loved the ranch, the dogs, cats, and horses. I went to a counselor afterwards and she had me write an anger letter to Jim. It took five anger letters to finally release all my frustration and fury. Then I read Louise Hay's book, *You Can Heal Your Life*. I drove in my car, screaming profanities at him. It felt good for the little Catholic girl to finally vent my anger.

The following year, I went to Santa Fe, New Mexico and met a Navajo psychic woman in a crystal shop. She said she still saw Jim in my aura and gave me a powerful mantra to release him. She told me to say this mantra every day for nine days.

Powerful mantra to release someone: "_____ (the person's name), I forgive you, bless you, and release you into the hands of the great spirit. I wish you well on your journey."

I gave myself a dignity bath each night saying this mantra. At that time, I was reading Shirley MacLaine's book, *Out On A Limb*.

On the ninth night of doing the mantra, I did one of Shirley MacLaine's meditation techniques in my bathtub with a candle burning. I said it so strongly and really meant it from the core of my being. I threw my hands in the air, exhaled, and the candle flickered as I breathed out. It had been a year since I left him, I'd read several self-help books, and done a lot of inner healing. I energetically moved away from him that night and identified this as another defining moment.

The next morning, I volunteered at a tree planting for Tree People in Hermosa Beach and I met my cute, new, tall, dark-haired boyfriend, Harry, while we planted a tree together. Harry was 10 years younger than me and was the perfect transitional boyfriend. God truly sent him to me so I could heal and move on.

Not saying goodbye to the kids I helped raise for 10 years, from their years of three until 13, I realized there were many key characters in my life to whom I never really said goodbye. I started thinking about all the people I've known and lost contact with. One was our family housekeeper, Minny Hawkins, who would come like clockwork every Friday to clean our big, old family home in Playa del Rey, California, for 20 years. She always did such a great job and I never had the chance to say goodbye to her. I never said goodbye to several good friends in my early twenties—fellow students and incredible artists at Art Center College of Design who graduated and moved to New York. Or my fellow art student friend, Howard, who died of a brain tumor. I often wonder about the bellmen and housekeepers from the Hyatt Los Angeles Hotel where I worked for three years as a concierge. Did I ever say goodbye to them? Or the many hotel sales managers and sales directors I worked with at various hotels around the world. Or Patty, the sweet sister of an old boyfriend. I never gave her a proper goodbye either.

Certain people really stand out. like George, a soulful, older friend who worked down the hall from me, who I used to have lunch with regularly. Where is he now? He has probably passed away. Do my other old friends ever think of me? When they cross my mind, is it because they're thinking of *me?* It hit me this morning that I could be seeing certain good friends *today* that for some reason I'll never see again. You just never know when a casual meeting with someone might be your last.

In Act 3, if we are more conscious of how precious each moment is, we can actually pause, take a deep breath, and speak from our hearts. We can tell our friends and family how much we love them, appreciate them, tell them the wonderful qualities that we notice in them, and acknowledge them. I've found that when I acknowledge the best qualities I see in others, they often touch their hearts and get tears in their eyes. The deepest desire of human nature is a craving to be appreciated.

I went to a hotel industry luncheon attended by about 55 of my colleagues one day; many of them were my good friends. As our lives take new twists and turns, how many people that day will I never see again? Knowing what I now understand about goodbyes and not writing people off, I treasured those friends and interactions in a more meaningful and mindful manner. I took a moment to look into people's eyes when I said goodbye; after all, you never know, that may be the last time.

You may tend to avoid goodbyes to avoid awkward moments of finality. Peter Pan said, "Never say goodbye because goodbye means going away and going away means forgetting." More often than not, it's an innocent oversight when you move on to something else, start a new job, graduate, or move away; the friendship just naturally faded away. As we get older and into our wow years, we can start to understand through the value of hellos, goodbyes, and the defining moments to shape our next act. We could ask, *What happened to our friendship? Was I a good enough friend?* It's important to go out of our way to say goodbye to important people. Sometimes we don't mean to not say goodbye. Sometimes we avoid this because we don't want it to be final. Do we have unfinished business with some key people?

Could I have written a note of appreciation to any of these friends if I was really conscious? Maybe I didn't want to acknowledge the finality of a relationship. If a person is gone and it's too late, maybe I could say goodbye to this person by writing in my journal or role playing with a friend. I could write the person a note or email, saying, "Here's what you mean or meant to me." It's a beautiful gesture. Who do you need some loving closure with? After all, "Every new beginning comes from some other beginnings' end" (From the song, "Closing Time" by Semisonic). *SEND LOVE*

Action step

Are there relationships in your life that feel unfinished? Any friendships that seem incomplete? Are there some people you'd still like to speak with? Do you feel a desire to appreciate or acknowledge someone special in your life? Some friends you'd like to contact or email? Do that now.

Recently, I had an incredible phone call from a friend. Barbara had always had a very tempestuous relationship with her Italian mother in upstate New York for her entire 60 years of life. She would always remark on how difficult this was for her. She said her 90-year-old mother just didn't understand her or even really seem to *like* her. Barbara was resigned to the fact that she always had a great, warm, loving relationship with her father who had just passed away, but a stormy, blusterous mother-daughter relationship prevailed throughout her life. Barbara could see that since her mother was so stubborn and outspoken, she would usually have a short, tense two- or three-day visit with her mother. Lately, her mother was mourning the death of her beloved soulmate-husband who passed away a year earlier. Once again, I was reminded that, "pain cracks you open so the light can get in" and the pain of missing her husband had softened her mother. One fall weekend, everything changed for them.

They had a truly transformative heart-to-heart talk. A healing occurred between them. The walls came down as her mother shared her vulnerable side and Barbara could see how the suffering and loss had made her mother grow. They hugged and cried together. Their mutual healing is a testament to the strength of the human spirit. Barbara said, "Rita, you can't give up on people." I saw more meaning in this quote: "Don't come to my funeral to show how much you cared about me. Show how much you care about me now...while I'm alive" (Unknown).

I have a friend who is always hanging up on people, judging them as unfit friends, blocking their cell phone numbers, and writing them off. We've all probably been tempted to write people off, and in some cases, it's very appropriate; for example, when there's abuse, betrayal, repeated ill treatment, disrespect, assault, etc.

When you're constantly writing people off, you don't end up with too many friends at the end of your life. You are holding yourself back from a wow life. It makes me wonder how many times friends were tempted to give up on me. When I stayed with the bad boyfriend way too long; when I went through whatever stage I was in at the time. We need to realize our friends and family have cut us slack, even though we hate to admit it.

I recently mended a friendship after a 20-year lapse. We met a month ago and both apologized to each other. It's just like old times now. We're picking up where we left off, but we're older, wiser, more compassionate, and it's a richer, deeper friendship now.

They say when you miss someone, you miss the person you are when you're with that person. We're all so unique, we can only be *that* person with them. Each friendship has its own personality; its own unique dynamic. With some friends we're fun and naughty, with others we're deep and soulful—and sometimes all of those with one person. But every friend or family member has special qualities we treasure and we feel life is richer because of them. They're like gems we collect along the way. As we love and accept our shadow and light, it's easier to forgive and accept the seeming flaws in others. If we reject our shadow, we reject those traits in others.

"A relationship is like a house. When a *light bulb* burns out, you don't go out and buy a new house, you fix the light bulb" (Unknown).

Action step

They say we meet a person for a season, a reason, or a lifetime. How many people in your whole life have you written off? Did some of those relationships feel unfinished? Were important words left unsaid? Could you possibly rekindle the friendship? Maybe it's actually perfect the way it ended, just as it is. Who ended the communication? Was there a possible misunderstanding? Ask yourself if it is time for some conscious endings or even a loving reconciliation.

When we forgive others, we forgive our own frailties and cut ourselves slack. Don't give up too soon on people you love. All that has shaped us from childhood to now is still part of who we are, but we now have the maturity and life experience to embrace and integrate the painful experiences and gain wisdom. We need to uncover limiting beliefs and emotional patterns that no longer serve us. Once we identify these beliefs and patterns, release them, and make behavior changes, we can fully experience our wow lives and feel joy in the present moment.

All this has shaped us from childhood and is probably still in play, but we have the maturity and life experience now to take hold of it in our wow lives and make behavior changes that could enhance our lives. Is this old, repetitive belief or feeling loving to you? No, this old feeling of fear or guilt is not loving to you, so it's time to interrupt the pattern. Commit to change. Now is the perfect time to break the old pattern, change course, redirect your life, and rehearse new traits.

Chapter Four

Like-aholism

Ahh, like-aholism. I have always been a like-aholic or a people-pleaser in my family from as far back as I can remember. Like-aholic—extracted from the word, alcoholic—is often facetious and sometimes refers to a person who is obsessed with being liked or has to like everything on Facebook. When I use this word, I mean people-pleaser. I love helping people get along with each other better and I truly enjoy making people happy. That trait served me well in the hospitality industry for many years…until it *didn't*. I was too accommodating in other areas, like in my love life. I was often afraid to speak up, make waves, cause too much conflict, or argue with friends or coworkers. That needed to change if I wanted to find a life partner to be with in my wow years. I also didn't need to be a doormat to friends or colleagues. I could use the tools I have learned in the last decades to construct better boundaries, yet still be the fullest me.

I was brought up with 12 years of Catholic education in a privileged, sheltered, upper-middle-class Los Angeles area beach community. There was something in the Catholic educational system that rewarded, reinforced, and encouraged the image of the good girl in me. At the core, people-pleasers really lack confidence because they yearn for outside validation.

Girls are trained from an early age to accommodate and defer to others. Our strict nuns in the old-fashioned black nuns' habits would measure the lengths of our school uniforms to make sure our skirts modestly touched our knees. Their castanets clicked to announce prayer intervals, time to genuflect, and un-questioningly recite church ideology from our catechisms. They taught us a mixed bag of religious dogma about belief in God, social responsibility, right and wrong, and the fact that sex was mostly sinful and only valid for marriage and procreation. I was trained to always do the right thing. I thought I must always put others before me. Phrases like "the meek shall inherit the earth" made a big impact on me.

No matter what I did, it never seemed good enough. Monthly visits to the priest's confessional usually resulted in me admitting or even fibbing that I'd (again) had impure thoughts and fought with my sister, just so I'd have sins to confess.

I always wanted the approval of my parents, teachers, and superiors. I figured I just liked to make people happy, even if it was at my expense; I must do nothing to upset others. As we talked in the previous chapter about inherited traits, I had no idea I was shaped this way. I could be a totally different person if I wanted. I just haven't known better, so I believed I must con-stantly work harder to make things better for others; I must not upset anyone. I was a middle child, so that made me a natural harmonizer, and this pattern of behavior served me well for much of my life. I was amiable, a good student, popular, and pretty well-adjusted. Even in my family as one of eight children, I remain a harmonizer, always helping keep the peace, and en-couraging everyone to get along.

By my early twenties, I noticed my people-pleasing was ex-treme. As a student at Art Center College of Design, I sensed that the college dean didn't like me for some reason. I would have a great day in class with all my friends but would drive home obsessing over why the grumpy old dean didn't like me. How could she not like *me*?

That's when I first realized I really wanted and needed to be liked by *everybody*. I was similar to Reese Witherspoon's character, Elle in the film, *Legally Blonde*, when she says about her new acquaintance at Harvard, "Wow! She doesn't like me?! How could she not like *me*? *Everyone* likes me!"

Action step

Do you feel a need to be liked by everyone? In what ways are you a people-pleaser? Do you constantly crave external validation? It's time to discover internal self-validation and build up what makes you feel good to increase your self-esteem.

Yes, being an approval junkie or people-pleaser only works for so long. It especially didn't serve me well in my thirties with my manipulative, commitment-phobic, live-in boyfriend, who was mainly just in it for himself. It also doesn't work while managing a staff of six people when you need to speak up to employees who are not doing their job or are treating you with disrespect. People-pleasing is putting others in the position of judge and jury as to your worthiness. In my forties, I learned and used the four-step conflict resolution process that I explained in chapter two. This process increased my ability to speak up and own my power. What helped me the most was learning to truly love myself. "The disease to please," as psychologist Harriet Braiker calls it, "is a form of addiction." As I loved myself more, I began to shift the focus from others to myself more often and stopped being a martyr to niceness. I finally left the 10-year dysfunctional, control-drama-filled relationship with my ex and realized that if people in my life weren't willing to accept that I have my own needs, they weren't worth having in my life. I learned how to diplomatically express myself. The willingness to help others needed to come after I learned how to help myself by expressing my own needs and desires.

Becoming obsessed with what others think about me is one of the fastest ways to lose my connection with the divine and myself.

If someone asked me in the past to do him or her a favor, my answer was usually yes. The seeds of people-pleasing are planted in childhood and from as far back as I can remember, I've been quite the people-pleaser. I realized that when I'm overwhelmingly honest about pleasing myself—ironically, I often end up pleasing others. Why is that? Could it be my energy shifts and thus becomes more congruent? I think I'm finally learning the difference between pleasing and loving. There's an energy shift in me when I'm pleasing myself—a purity.

My favorite tips for recovering like-aholics like me

1. Take small steps—do you have trouble saying no and setting boundaries? Try saying no with small steps, like suggesting an alternative activity; for example, I really don't care for baby showers, so if I get invited to a baby shower and the person is a good friend, I often say I can't make the baby shower, but I'd love to take that friend to lunch and I give her a baby gift over lunch.

2. Rehearse loving yourself enough to say no. Instead of "fake it 'til you make it," fake it 'til you *become* it. Mentally rehearse the new action you want. Mentally rehearse saying no. Teach your body ahead of time; shift your frequency from low self-esteem to a higher love frequency. Start *feeling* worthy, feeling whole, loving yourself, and loving others. Your thoughts and feelings are outcomes of life. Feel like a person with self-esteem, then become it. Feel better; feel what the future will feel like ahead of the experience. You can *choose* when to say yes and when to say no; you're no longer a victim.

3. Suggest another time that works for you. Suggest a timeframe that works for you; for instance, "Sure. I can help you from 4:00pm to 6:00pm." I had a friend who was constantly asking me to babysit her children. I loved her kids, but I found that time limits worked better for me.

4. What if it's your boss? When I worked for a large corporation, I had to confront an intimidating boss about an error she made. This boss had published the wrong sales figures for my Los Angeles office, which made us look like we were underperforming. She knew she made the error and was not expecting me to challenge her. It was new for me to speak up, so I wrote up some notes, practiced what I had to say, and made an appointment to speak to her. She was very surprised at my new assertiveness and she sent out an email to everyone in the company correcting the error.

5. Don't give too many excuses. Just be simple in your explanation. If you try too hard to defend yourself, it usually backfires.

6. Delay your response—stall. Say, "Hmm...I think there's something on my calendar. Let me get back to you tomorrow." I learned a fun way to honestly say no to people who ask me favors when I know I really need a day to myself to rejuvenate or rest. I say, "Sorry, I have something on the calendar that day." Guess whose name is on the calendar? My own. I put my name on the calendar when I need a pajama day to rest, take a bath in Epsom salts, light a candle, read inspirational books, or get my nails done. *I'm* on my calendar so it's not even a white lie.

7. Be selective about romantic people pleasing—too much people pleasing and hiding true feelings can

sabotage your love relationships. Honor your truth and be brave with your partner. Subjugating your desires to those of your romantic partner disconnects both of you and eventually comes out in the long run. The energy actually expands between you and your partner when you share your truth with each other.

8. Check in with your intuition or your heart—when someone asks for a favor or wants you to do something, instead of immediately saying yes, check in, take a deep breath, and center yourself. If your heart sinks or you feel a *clunk,* say no or delay by saying, "I think I might have something on my calendar." Ask for time to think about it before giving an answer. If your heart soars and you feel aliveness and the energy is expansive, say yes.

9. Set healthy boundaries—What about if you feel pressed to do something for someone because you are afraid if you don't, they will go away or stop calling? I know for me, I have to fully love myself completely to know what boundaries and values I have for loving someone, or being respected in a romantic relationship. Set boundaries about what you can and cannot do and what you will and will not accept, and then stick to it. We teach the world how to treat us, and the world around us changes when we change.

10. Rehearse what you need to say. What if something is just plain unacceptable? It takes practice and determination to unlearn old, habitual, people-pleasing behavior, so be realistic and realize you may need to rehearse what you are going to say. Sometimes I have to write notes prior to a difficult conversation. I have a couple good friends who help me rehearse what I need to say when I have to set a new, healthy boundary. Here's

another good response: What if someone is continuously inconsiderate and repeatedly cancels at the last minute? "I'm sorry to hear you can't make it. I understand things come up, but I've got so much going on these days, I wish I could have been informed sooner so I could have made alternate plans. Hope we can reschedule."

It has taken me many years to be okay with pleasing myself. My friendships are much more balanced these days in my Act 3, with give and take being a two-way street. They are like figure eights with energy flowing back and forth in more of a balance. This doesn't mean I don't still ask myself what I did wrong. If someone doesn't call me back right away, I think, "I wonder if she's mad at me" at least a few times a month. I guess old habits die hard and you could say I'm still a recovering like-aholic. Loving myself a little more each day and speaking up for myself is still a challenge at times. I still have setbacks when people and situations bring me back to an old paradigm I think I've broken from, but I'm grateful for even subtle shifts. Our job is to be uncomfortable and to grow. We're *all* works in progress and it may sound selfish, but it does have to start with me first, then that self-love will naturally flow out to others, so can I do that favor for you? Hmmm...let me check my calendar and I'll get back to you.

Action step

Are you a people pleaser? If so, how can you prepare for the next time you feel you may cave in and respond in like-aholic mode? Planning ahead to use some of these tips can help you brace yourself for the next time someone asks you to do an obnoxious favor that you will regret doing. I especially like the stall technique. If they catch you off-guard, you can say, "Let me get back to you tomorrow on that." Prepare for the next request. Write down your own like-aholic tendencies and your favorite tips now.

Consistently putting others' needs above your own can have bad consequences. If pulling out of the cycle seems overwhelming, identify one small like-aholic tendency you'd like to change and work from there. Do things that resonate with you and act in accordance with your highest values and principles. Nipping this in the bud will help you have a much more satisfying wow life. It's time to be true to you.

Chapter Five

Navigating Relationships
in the Wow Years

Deborah was in a long-term, unhealthy, rollercoaster relationship until she woke up one day and said, "Enough!" Contrary to her parents' loving, 55-year marriage, her live-in boyfriend, Matt, was everything her role model father was not. He was unreliable, manipulative, financially unstable, erratic, and unfaithful. Choosing to break up with Matt and be single in her mid-fifties in Los Angeles was troubling, but she wisely opted for self-love and self-care. She had attended one of my workshops and had done powerful exercises to release what wasn't working.

While her mind, body, and soul needed the change, Deborah was less than enthusiastic to jump back into the dating world. Friends encouraged her to be brave and open to love and she reluctantly joined a popular online dating site. Months later, at an impromptu dinner with a good friend, she shared that internet dating was not for her and she was removing her profile from the site. Her friend quickly said, "Hang in there! That is how I met my boyfriend!" She heeded her friend's advice and decided to give it more time. Within one week, she met her soulmate, Dan, and two years later they are planning their wedding and new life. They mutually love, adore, respect each other and are kindred spirits on all levels.

Your Wow Years

Don't be afraid to move on to find new love in your wow years; they are some of your most solid years where you have a handle on who you are and can finally attract a soulmate who is fully aligned with you.

We've lived a few decades by now, each age bringing forth a different set of experiences and outlooks. We have friendships and work-related, business relationships that may no longer serve us. If a long-term job is ending, you realize you have to change the ways you meet people. You may be entering your wow years in an already-established marriage, divorced, or looking for that special someone again.

If you are starting your wow years with new partners, you may be worried how much of a hold the old agendas have on you.

Along with hellos and goodbyes, there are and could continue to be in-between stages. I know for me, personally, in those transitional periods, I have wondered when I will ever get it right. *Will I attract the right person this time around?* Don't make yourself wrong for the choices you made prior to these years, because they were all informative about who you want to be in a relationship now.

Moving on...

During your wow years, you realize that time is precious, and you don't want to waste a single minute with the wrong person. A few years ago, an ex-boyfriend came back into my life and I noticed that the more time I spent with him, the less I loved myself. He ended up really hurting me again and I felt stranded and bereft. I needed someone to pour my heart out to, but no one was available. I took out my journal and scribbled the whole, sad saga onto page after page. I found that writing unleashed my pent-up emotions and tears spilled down my cheeks onto the pages of my journal. I was crying so hard that the tears blurred

58

my vision. Something happened towards the end of this outpouring; I felt relief and then a catharsis. I released so many repressed emotions and finally started to breathe easier. My tirade against this old flame had cleansed me and I felt so much better. I was surprised at the deep feelings I still felt about this man. It seems like there had been some unfinished business between us and I obviously loved him more than I'd ever been honest enough to admit. I must have had a blind spot about him and had never been honest enough to admit my true feelings.

As he broke my heart again, our relationship was really over this time. I'm embarrassed to say he was a bit clueless and pretty wounded by his last marriage; and he hadn't truly healed yet. He just wasn't there for me when I needed him and he did not show up for me. I realized I just didn't have time for it anymore. Under the sadness, I uncovered my pure, open heart and knew I would love again. It's important to honor every relationship—grieve them if necessary—and not make ourselves wrong for the choices we made so that we don't look back with regret or anger. I decided that next time I'd communicate more openly and honestly right from the beginning and I'd seek a man with scars but not so many open wounds.

Action step

Is there a person who is sucking the soul from your life? Be discerning. Don't hang on too long. Have you had enough?

What can you *now* release?

Maybe it's time to raise your standards. Write down anyone who is draining you with behavior that you are no longer willing to accept in your life.

Write down the behavior you will no longer tolerate:

I am now raising my standards and accepting the following:

Now that you've identified the people you want to remove from your life, we will work on bringing in the people who are positive.

I'm sure you've heard the phrase, "Fall in love with yourself." In your wow years, you can fall in love with yourself all over again. In fact, it's vital that you do this before you call in someone else. I said to a friend the other day, in learning to love myself, I went from "I like me, I like who I'm becoming" to "I love me, I love who I'm becoming, and who I've become." I'm a catch and I'd be honored to date me; in fact, I'm at a stage where I'd *love* to date me! If you send out the signal, "I love me and I love who I *am*," that love will flow out to others. When you're in love with your life and yourself, you'll create an equal. Set an intention to meet a high-quality partner and create an index card with "I love me! I am (list your positive traits here: beautiful, desirable, magnetic, powerful, irresistible, etc.) and I can have what I want," etc.

Now that you've done the crucial work of clearing the field for your perfect mate, here are some other steps you can do. Write down all the qualities you want in your next mate. Show up, be your full self, and stop worrying about other people's feelings. Identify your fears around attracting a new relationship. One of my realizations as a recovering like-aholic is that we're not going to learn it all at once. I was still worrying too much about the feelings of other guys even when I knew I had to move on. We haven't learned it all. At our age, we still have a lot of old conditioning to unravel.

Thoughts are electric and feelings are magnetic, so get out there and broadcast a strong, clear signal to others that you're open and available. When you resonate at a high frequency, you'll move forward in a heart-centered way and attract other high frequency people. Love yourself more and more every day. Soon you'll be amazed at the other loving people in your life who are on a similar path, interested in growth and expansion as much as you. Are you the type of person with whom you'd like to spend the rest of your life? As you grow in self-love and acceptance, you'll honestly soon be saying, "OMG, I'd *love* to date me!"

If you seek stimulating activities, conferences, and events, you will meet other interesting people like yourself. When you step up and are open to learning and embracing exciting, new ideas, you'll meet other people on a similar path; people who are as interested in growth and expansion as you.

We attract through resonance. We don't attract *what we want,* we attract *who* we *are.* Resonance is fascinating. "The law of resonance, which is closely interconnected and works in harmony with the law of attraction is the universal law that determines precisely what it is you will attract into your life based on the resonance or frequency of the energy that you are projecting" (www.abundanceandhappiness.com). As I mentioned in chapter two, as our vibration grows more positive with our capacity to give and understand what we need, the universe brings us equally high-vibrational people who will nurture us and truly *get* what we are giving them; they are aligned with us. Invest time with those people who nurture and appreciate you. Appreciation appreciates. To battle the daunting self-talk that prevents you from aspiring to your dreams in your wow years, spend time with people who are uplifted with a spirit of love and daring, and be ruthless about cutting people out of your life who are negative or toxic. There's a distinction between people who are negative or toxic and people who give us good, solid, realistic advice. It's not just having yes-people in our lives. There's a distinction between people who spend a significant amount of time focused on the unwanted things in life and those who get stuck on a track of negativity that is hard to shift. Toxic people are manipulative, judgmental, and take no responsibility for their own feelings. They don't apologize, are inconsistent, and make you defend yourself.

They're draining, and after time with them you feel emotionally wiped out. Remove yourself from their ploys or traps. Distance yourself from them emotionally. Friends who give you loving, kind, honest feedback and solid, realistic advice can be most beneficial and invaluable.

Giving and receiving is like a figure eight flowing back and forth, affirming self-love, mutual love, and respect for each other. As a professional life coach, I enjoy this quote: "When the teacher is ready, the students appear!" This is another way of saying I'm attracting students who are a vibrational match.

Consciously investing your precious time and energy is vital to getting the most out of your wow years. In order to do this, ask yourself some key questions:

Do I feel exhausted after I spend time with certain people?

Am I using my soul's energy to expand or contract?

Am I over-giving in this relationship?

Is this person open to my energy or do I feel drained after I'm with this person?

Does this relationship serve my highest truth?

Does it serve my highest choice to give this gift?

When you're giving your time and energy to someone, ask yourself if it is too big a gift for this person. Is it too much for you to offer them your gifts of time, advice, or services?

Consider boundary issues. Mix these human dynamics with practical, highly-evolved methods of handling this. Be practical *and* spiritual. Once you determine whether the person is open to change, offer solutions to stir people to come up with their *own* solutions—practical soul solutions. One of the best life coaches I know constantly asks her clients, "What do *you* think you should do now?" She consciously listens to them and coaches the solution out of them and they then truly commit and buy into the solution, since they were an active part of the process.

Now that you have identified what's bothering you and you're resonating with a higher vibration, it's time for shadow work. The shadow is a psychological term for "everything we can't see in ourselves," according to Scott Jeffrey, who adds, "It's always standing right behind us, just out of view. In any direct light, we cast a shadow." Growing is easy when you're by yourself. When you live alone, you don't have someone pointing out your faults as often, so you don't necessarily see your shadow. Your spouse, partner, or children tend to point out your faults and best skills. I recall in my last relationship, my boyfriend pointed out that I didn't listen to him very well. Ugh! I was so surprised when he said that, but I knew he was right. I knew sometimes I would daydream while he was talking. In what way are we not really listening to others? I'm learning more and more to practice presence when others are speaking, offering reverent alertness and being more conscious of listening.

Action step

Ask a friend to try this listening exercise with you.

1. First time around—talk to another person for a minute about something you are excited about. Tell him or her to ignore you, to not really listen, rudely look around, and check his or her cell phone.

2. Second time around—once again, talk about something you're passionate and excited about, but ask him or her to listen with undivided, rapt attention, excitement, and alertness. Notice how both people feel after each of these exercises. It's fascinating how on the second time around, both speaker and listener are excited and honored by the attention given. This presence given to each other is such an important part of a relationship; such a gift to each other.

Connect

63

Clearing the air

Speaking of listening and practicing presence with each other, I've found a new communication tool that has really helped me in my relationships and friendships. It's a small step in practicing more presence with people and can make a big difference, depending on the situation. If I accidentally say something to a friend and it just doesn't sound right upon reflection, or I think I may have inadvertently offended or hurt the person, I quickly address the issue or call him or her back to clarify the conversation or apologize. This is a recent change in my behavior. In the past, I might have let the conversation pass by without saying anything more, even though it didn't sit quite right with me and I probably had hurt the person's feelings; I might have shrugged and tried to gloss over it.

The other day, my friend, Katie, and I had a phone conversation. We hung up and she called me right back. She said, "I'm sorry if I sounded ungrateful for what you did for me and I just wanted to explain." She went on to clarify the situation and it truly did make a difference. I've now done this twice with two other friends since then; something went clunk when I hung up and I sensed there was a misunderstanding, so each time I called the friend right back. I quickly cleared the air and both friends really appreciated the loving gesture I took to clarify the situation. The quick apology smoothed over what could have been a lasting rift due to miscommunication.

Why not take that extra step the next time you feel strange, or a bit off, when you end a conversation? You might be opening a can of worms, so if you do call back, be prepared; however, in the long run, you'll be glad you showed the openness, humility, and vulnerability to apologize. Try this the next time your intuition says your friend may have misunderstood what you just said.

Your quick apology and clarification just might spare hurt feelings and even save a very dear friendship.

The bottom line is we all are human beings who want to be loved and seen and heard by a loved one, so putting energy into attracting a suitable mate is a noble act in the wow years. That said, the key to being fulfilled and complete the rest of your life is continuing to work on making *you* a better person, regardless of who you attract.

Chapter Six

Releasing Old Self-talk
and Living by Default

The quality of conversations you have with yourself determines the quality of your life. How many times did you praise yourself today? How many times do you praise others during the day? Are you aware of the chatter and conversation going on in your head? It's a mixed bag at best. If you ever really focused on the way you talk to yourself, you'd be so much more kind. Deepak Chopra says 85-90% of what you say to yourself every day is negative and repetitive. I'm working on getting my negative chatter down and it takes real, focused effort. Here's a sample of my inner dialog from the other day:

"Why did I say that? I wonder if he's mad at me? What did I do wrong? I can't believe I did that. What could he be thinking? He was so inconsiderate." Then after a nice get together: "That was fun. It really turned out well. I really enjoyed that. Sue is so nice. Now, what? I think I'm making progress. I deserve a pat on the back. Time for some self-praise. You're doing so well." At the end of the day: "That was a powerful meditation this morning. Good for you! You ate so healthy today. So glad I exercised; happy I gave my brother moral support tonight; he needed that. Did I allow my thoughts to go down a negative road too much today? Did I talk too much? Was I a conscious listener? How could I have practiced being more present with others today?" Before I go to sleep: "I'm proud of you. I love how you stretch yourself to change and grow every day."

Inner chatter is a mixed bag at best. Scientists say our negativity bias stems from our survival instinct, which is always on guard for the ubiquitous threats in our life. We're hard wired to be aware of danger in order to keep us safe. Unlearning the negative inner chatter and fear-based, limiting beliefs takes time and practice. You wouldn't talk to your worst enemy the way you often speak to yourself.

My 55-year-old friend, Susan, is in real estate and she strives to keep her mood at a high, positive level in order to navigate her volatile, competitive real estate business. She manages so many variables that are out of her control every day. Every morning, Susan meditates using the Deepak Chopra/Oprah meditation experience, then says affirmations as she walks the beach. She takes videos of the waves, then watches and listens to the videos later. When she feels empty or nervous, the ocean videos energize her and get her mind into a more peaceful place. Her clients are often super stressed, since their lives are in transition. Susan may have her challenges going on, but she can't show this, since her clients need her calm, positive support.

She likes to say positive affirmations like this one on her walks: "I expand in love, success, and abundance every day as I inspire those around me to do the same."

If I can impress anything upon you today, remember to praise yourself often during the day and then compliment others. Be *kind* to yourself. Imagine yourself as a loving child who tries so hard every day, and say, "You did so well today."

Have you noticed some inner chatter holding you back from being the best you could be? Many of your limiting beliefs that hold you back from manifesting your desires came up in the last chapter. In this chapter, you'll learn some tools to get out of this stuck state. There are many ways we talk ourselves out of stretching, growing, and being the best version of who we are, and this inhibits us from a truly wow life in our Act 3. In your journal each morning after you ask, "What would my soul love to do today?" If you notice negative chatter going on in your head, you can then write the next question, "What's bothering me?" This is an Abraham-Hicks technique. We all have inner, repetitive, mostly negative chatter going on in our head. Since this question is broad, I suggest you also make a more specific list of what's bothering you:

1. What in your life is feeling stagnant?
2. Who got on your nerves recently?
3. Where are you not making forward movement?
4. How did someone hurt your feelings?
5. Any additional bothers, like you got some disappointing news, you gained two pounds, you're lonely, have relationship problems...?

No matter how positive you usually are or how much you love your job or your spouse, bad days happen to the best of us. Miraculously, the moment you label and name what is going on in your life, you *begin to feel the breakthrough miracle*. Even neuroscience backs this activity up as a reliable way to shift a person's mindset about a problem. A study at UCLA said that just the act of writing down and labeling negative emotions, such as anger and sadness, decreased the person's anxiety and negative response. Similarly, labeling your problems will help you feel better about them because even just a few words about your issue activates the prefrontal cortex to reduce the dark emotions while stimulating the problem-solving area of your brain. It really works. Making this list causes breakthrough moments because it feels like someone tossed you a flashlight; even though you might still be in a hole, at least you can now see!

Who needs your love today? → *Double Edge*

One sure fire way to get out of your own negative emotions and limited thinking is to consider others. Ask yourself who needs your love and you will quickly think of someone you know. You can check in with the person energetically or reach out via email, text, or phone if you feel they need some love and support. Don't you love when someone you care about checks in to see how you're doing?

You may even think of someone who annoys you or someone you are having communication issues with and find out the issue with them could also be an issue *you* have; this is why he or she is triggering your irritation response. Today, I was annoyed that a good friend of mine never wants to talk on the phone, yet he will constantly text me during the day. Even when I leave him a voicemail, he'll just text back. Texting is perfect for short messages, but it is a very limited form of communication. Could he be subconsciously avoiding intimacy? I asked myself, *I wonder what's going on with him that I don't know about?*

Now, I take the focus from picking him out as a problem and I go back to the self. Ask, in what way am I also similar to this person? What's this reflecting to me about me? How do I put up barriers, play it safe, and avoid intimacy? When you judge or reject something in yourself, you can't stand it in other people. Identify the flaw because you may also have it. It bugs you more when you also have the same fault. This inner chatter holds you back from fully having your wow now. Writing about these issues and clearing them in your journal can clean your energy field for a fully wow day and a wow life. Maybe *you* need more love today. Are you loving yourself as you would wish another to love you?

"We don't see things as they are; we see them as *we* are" (Anais Nin).

Here's an extreme case. I knew an interesting, wealthy, well-traveled woman in her mid-seventies named Veronica. She was in a women's group of 14 women. If she perceived that someone was flawed, she dismissed them and wrote them off. She would say, "(The person's name) is not evolved at all; we can't have her in our group." She eventually thought the women I brought into the group (including me) weren't worthy. One by one, she rejected each of these women for various faults, and in the end, she had "assassinated" 13 of them. She got down to the two most highly evolved leaders in the group. She finally wrote one group leader off, but is still in contact with the other group leader. Members of the group called her the Assassinator. She eventually dropped out of the group because she ultimately judged most of us as flawed or unworthy. She continued to write people off in her life and is done with them because they didn't live up to her unspoken, hidden rules or standards. Was this due to her lack of self-love and self-acceptance? Was she actually rejecting herself? We usually judge others in the areas where we feel the weakest. We judge others harshly because we do the same to ourselves. Do you see any of this in you? Do you do this on a smaller scale? Are you "assassinating" friends who you judge as flawed, yet are honestly seeing the same traits in yourself? Are you believing you're better than other people? An interesting update on Veronica is that she has recently moved back to Los Angeles after some big life lessons and she's been reaching out, wanting to reconnect with a spiritual group of women friends. She is actually in a more humble, open, compassionate frame of mind.

Take heed; when we judge others, we can go deeper and ask in what ways we are also doing this. Be ready for possible revelations, openings, and connections. Problems can be openings, portals, or doors to new insights.

"When you judge others, you do not define them; you define yourself" (Earl Nightingale).

We cannot change what we will not acknowledge. When we are self-aware, we can acknowledge our weaknesses, make the necessary changes, and move forward. A new way to perceive what bothers us is to become curious and stay out of judgment; for example, ask yourself why this bothers you so much. Why do you have such a hot button or charge about it?

A few years ago, I read about a woman executive who had a big corporate position in senior management in New York City. She was standing at the podium ready to speak to a group of professional peers and as she was about to speak, she suddenly felt like an imposter posing as a successful executive. She thought, *I wonder when they're going to discover it's only me?* I'm not really this big, successful, corporate leader. This feeling is called "the imposter syndrome. Wikipedia says, "Imposter syndrome can be defined as a collection of feelings of inadequacy that persist even in the face of information that indicates the opposite is true."

I read about an Academy-Award-winning director who once said his biggest fear was that people would find out he was a fake. He had already won an Oscar!

I felt like an Imposter 19 years ago when I created my new company, Elite Resorts & Spas. We brought a group of 25 meeting planners up to Ojai Valley Inn & Spa to familiarize them with the resort and show them the recent hotel renovation, so they'd book corporate meetings at the resort. A large sign on an easel next to our cocktail reception said, "Elite Resorts & Spas—Welcome Reception." It was the first time I'd ever seen my company name so prominently displayed. I gulped, *Yikes! What if they find out Elite Resorts & Spas is only* me? No one knew how I felt, so I just acted as if this was all very normal for me. I was scared and excited. My voicemail at that time said, "We're not in right now, but we'll get back to you when we receive this message." The we at the time was my big orange, fluffy cat, Taffey, and me, but my services were larger than life.

We experience this syndrome over and over again when we're advancing to higher levels of achievement in life. They say, "Fake it till you make it," but I asked myself *how will I know when I've made it?* Every time I accomplish a goal, there's always another bigger goal on the next horizon. I never seem to get there. Where's there? There's no "there" there anyway. Why do so many gifted people, especially women, feel like they're imposters, in spite of their success?

We're all imposters, actors, pretenders, and role players at different times in our lives, until we fully integrate and embody our true authentic self and learn to love and appreciate ourselves as our higher selves. Act *as if* you're already there. Wear it like empress robes—regal new clothing. Eventually, you are not faking it. When you do the same work after many years of practice, you often feel like, *I finally get it.* Malcolm Gladwell says in his bestseller, *The Outliers: The Story of Success*, that it takes roughly 10,000 hours in a subject to be an expert or to achieve mastery in a field. That's about 90 minutes a day for 20 years of practice, when one becomes an outlier. He says, "Ten thousand hours is the tipping point of greatness."

Accept and forgive the part of you that holds onto the imposter energy. You're really a Christed being who walks the Earth. What you're working on becoming, you already *are*. As Eckhart Tolle says, "You get there by realizing you're already there." And the sky's the limit.

Knowing all our inner resistance is at play, how can you make a shift and start your day off in a more positive way? When you wake in the morning, thank God or your higher power for at least five blessings in your life. Thanking God or the universe raises your vibration and increases your abundance. Those people who aren't noticing the gifts coming into their lives really

72

miss out. Those gifts will diminish after a while if they're not acknowledged because what we focus on expands and what we don't appreciate goes away. A powerful affirmation to write and say is: "I boldly break through all barriers for the joy-filled manifestation of my soul's purpose. All is well in my world!"

Saying, "Thank you, thank you, thank you!" actually raises your vibration.

Action step

I recently did a workshop with women in their fifties and this exercise instantly brought up their unconscious, limiting beliefs that were blocking them from achieving some of their goals.

Exercise—my dreams are now coming true

Example: To have an amazing relationship with my soulmate/spouse/life partner

Write on the left-hand side of the paper:

"My dreams are now coming true."

On the right-hand side of the paper, write any responses or resistance that comes up:

"But I can't have this type of relationship because I don't even know if it's possible."

Continue the exercise by writing down on the left-hand side of the page ten times, "My dreams are now coming true," with responses that come up on the right-hand side of the page. Write until you don't get any more feelings of resistance or new responses. In the end of the exercise, you should start truly feeling, *Yes, my dreams* are *now coming true!*

Have you felt some shifts so far? Back in chapter one, I encouraged you to take this leap to access a greater life through this work and put more wow into your now. In chapter two, I encouraged you to do something brave, bold, and new every day to increase your brain's neuroplasticity. In chapter three, we discussed worthiness and feeling enough. In chapter four, we looked back on like-aholism and people pleasing. Are you now ready to clean up some old, negative programs? As I mentioned earlier, we think sixty- to seventy-thousand thoughts a day and 85-90% of those thoughts are negative and repetitive. Old limiting beliefs repeat over and over in our heads. You would never talk to another person the mean-spirited way you sometimes talk to yourself.

The following are some of the sample self-limiting belief statements I hear from my clients. Regardless of whether you are in business for yourself, working for an employer, or retired, these limiting beliefs can apply to your life.

1. The competition is so tough, it's hard to get clients to say yes.
2. I'm just not motivated.
3. I'm not good enough.
4. I'm afraid to say what I really feel.
5. It's hard to find a nice guy/woman at my age.
6. I'm not worthy of asking for more money.
7. I'll look foolish. (I'm too old, I don't know enough.)

Write your limiting belief statement here:

The goal is to replace these limiting statements with new wow-now go-to thoughts and programs which will help you think fresh, liberating thoughts. Turn these old limiting programs around and create new go-to, empowering programs like these.

What are some new wow-now go-to thoughts you can use? I have a lot of fun with my go-to thoughts because for me, now living into my wow years, I can play and have fun with the possibilities.

Here are some wow-now go-to thoughts:

1. I have the resources to generate abundant streams of revenue from sources known and unknown. My good is now coming to me.
2. I am now getting in touch with my passion and am excited to grow and learn. I'm ready to make this my best, most awesome chapter of life ever.
3. I have all the skills, talents, knowledge, experience, and wisdom to have the most satisfying year of my life.
4. I focus on passion and service; as I speak my heart, my passion shines through. I communicate with honesty and diplomacy.
5. I'm now experiencing a happy, fulfilling marriage *or* there are many available men/women to date and I'm now attracting my perfect mate/life partner.
6. I am worthy and making abundant income. Money is now flowing to me from sources known and unknown.
7. I am courageous as I do something bold, brave, and new every day. What did you do today?

Action step

Although you can use my sample wow-now go-to thoughts for as long as you would like, I would like you to create your own original thoughts:

Write your new wow-now go-to thoughts here:

Negative thoughts are like Velcro that sticks to us due to our survival instincts. Positive thoughts are like Teflon and they slide off easier, so we need to repeat positive affirmations daily in order to counteract, reinforce, and reprogram old, negative patterns. Affirmations are so powerful. There was a time in my life when I did not feel pretty, so I decided to tell myself over and over, "I feel pretty, I feel pretty, I feel pretty." On one of those down days, I was wearing a red top and a jean skirt. I was thinking, I hate this outfit and when I get home tonight, I'm going to throw it in the trash. I decided to really test out this new affirmation. I was in the Santa Monica shopping mall and I said my affirmation, "I feel pretty," repeatedly as I walked through the perfume department; a woman looked at me and said, "You're very pretty." I thought, "Wow, this works!" I walked into the outdoor part of the mall and a man on a park bench nodded at me and said, "Very pretty." I loved it! I kept repeating, "I feel pretty," and another man came up to me and said, "Excuse me. May I have your phone number? You are very pretty!" I had such a big smile. "OMG! I love how powerful affirmations are." That weekend, I was on a roll, so I decided to try a new affirmation: "I'm vibrant, magnetic, and irresistible to the opposite sex." I went to a party that Saturday night and two men asked me out. I promise you, this stuff works!

Tear up your old limiting beliefs and repeat your new go-to liberating beliefs daily.

Here's another powerful technique that releases old negative programs that I like to call The *Until-Now* Habit Breaker Exercise. Sometimes, we mindlessly repeat negative affirmations for bad habits by casually using the powerful words, "always" and "never." I'll be walking with friends who will say, "I *always* give up on my diet after I've lost a couple pounds. I figure I can start eating again," or, "I *never* have enough confidence to look for a new job." These are negative affirmations.

The following until-now habit-breaker exercise creates new neural pathways in your brain and helps you break old, worn out habits. What old always- or never-phrases would you like to let go? Some examples of subconscious, old, negative always- and never-phrases you can now release are:

- I *always* attract bad types of men/women who mistreat me and don't respect me.
- I *always* eat too many salty snacks at parties.

- I *always* overeat during the holidays.
- I *never* have enough confidence to talk to strangers at networking events or parties.
- I *never* feel good enough.
- I *never* have the courage to speak up about my true feelings.

The good news is, once you recognize an old, disempowering phrase, you can stop it. You don't need to say that anymore, so when you clean it up, it's going to stay clean. You truly can stop the negative from creeping back in. I've seen this exercise work miracles with so many people. What always- and never-, negative, disempowering phrases do you often say?

Action step

Write the phrase you'd like to release here:

I always _____.

Then put your hands up like a crossing guard with a stop sign and say, *"until now!"*

Write another phrase you'd like to release here:

I never _____

Then put your hands up like a stop sign and say, *"until now!"*

Hold your hands out like a crossing guard indicating a stop sign. Say the old negative phrase and say, *"until now!"* Done. No more! Do you feel this breakthrough moment? Now that you're aware you mindlessly repeat these old, negative phrases for years, you don't need to do it anymore. My friends on the walks? They know now to expect me to hold up my hands and say, *"until now!"* to their negative phrases. We always laugh. Once you see how disempowering an old phrase is, you don't need to do it anymore! This exercise is a very powerful, effective habit breaker. The physicality of your hands indicating stop-signs can change neural pathways; it's a double re-enforcer.

Your wow years are too precious to be brought down by the weight of the old, self-limiting beliefs and negative self-talk. Will you save the world, work on some of your pet causes, semi-retire, take time to develop some of your talents or hobbies that have been put on the back-burner, or simply retire? What feels right for you? To have the most wonderful Act 3 of your life, take some time for self-reflection, writing out a life review, and you may discover a lot of things that happened weren't your fault. You've gained wisdom and you're learning how to respond differently. You may you go back, reflect, and reframe what happened so you now have positive feelings about the past. You can move into this phase of your life clean from the past and full of new passion and purpose for your future. Study your Act 1 and Act 2. *Who was I really? Who do I aspire to become?* I'm going to be asking more questions in the road map of preparation. Will you bring a new you to the table? How can you use these years to make a difference? Act 3 is the most important act, after all. I love to say, "Your best wow is yet to come!"

Chapter Seven
Plan Your Escape

I coached Paul, a computer analyst in the defense industry whose secret desire was to work in computer animation. Paul was working at a mind-numbing, technical job in the defense industry in Arizona and he really wanted to work for a top animation company in Los Angeles. According to Gallup, only 30% of American workers are satisfied in their jobs. Statistically, Paul was one of those in the 70% of Americans who are disengaged, stuck in a boring job, and perplexed about what to do to lean into a new career. Paul's dream was to be a part of creating inspiring, uplifting films. We diagramed his ideal career from the type of work to travel, to friends and family. Everything unfolded quickly. Within a week after we worked together on his perfect job, he had a springboard job working for a small visual effects company in Hollywood. A year later, he was working at Walt Disney Animation Studios on films like *Wreck-It Ralph, Frozen 1 and 2* and *Moana*. It's now a few years later and he just finished his latest blockbuster Disney film. The plan we outlined manifested and he's so grateful. Paul is now in the 30% of workers who actually *love* what they are doing for a living.

Is it time for you in your wow years to plan your escape from where you are? Lean in or modify your new career? Design your next act? Yes—get ready to transition into your next, most awesome phase of life.

In the year 2000, I was working as a regional director of sales for a very upscale, luxury hotel corporation promoting group business to these properties. It was a plum job with a large corner office on Wilshire Blvd in Los Angeles. I visited 90 four- and five-star hotels and resorts around the world in six years. I had reached one of the highest positions in my industry and even won a cruise in my final year there for being top salesperson. When I went to book the cruise, the hotel company reneged on the prize they'd promised me. They said they couldn't give me the cruise because my boss never got approval for it, but they would check into getting me a discount on a cruise. Ugh! So. Not. Fair! But there was a gift in this challenge; a blessing in the adversity. You may be skeptical when you read this but because of that, I started planning my escape from this corporation, which was one of the best decisions I've ever made. This job was very stressful and I often felt like a rat on a treadmill.

Speaking of treadmills, my state of mind corresponded beautifully with a couple hamsters and a trip to visit my brother's house in Carlsbad. The only available bedroom was my eight-year-old niece's room, which was also home to three very cute, little hamsters. I thought, *No problem; I like hamsters. I'll be able to sleep in the same room as these cute, furry, little creatures.*

Wrong! I never realized hamsters were nocturnal. Almost immediately, one of the little darlings jumped on his hamster wheel and started energetically running around and around. As I tossed and turned, listening to that frantic pitter-patter, I thought *OMG! when is that little dude going to take a* breather? Hours went by— round and round and round he went on his little blue treadmill. It was torture trying to sleep. I couldn't tell if the three hamsters were trading off, taking turns jumping on and off the wheel, or if it was the same one furiously running round and round for hours. Whew... I put a pillow over my head in a futile attempt to block out the incessant, whirling sound.

What could possibly make these animals run like that for so many hours? As I lay there trying to sleep, I started thinking, *Is this a metaphor for my life?* They talk about how running on a hamster wheel describes people who keep running in circles and making the same mistakes over and over, instead of progressing.

In desperation, I got up at 3:35am, gathered my belongings, and made the two-hour trek home. As I drove home on the 5 freeway north, I thought, *it's definitely time to program some new thoughts into my life. Time to jump off* my *hamster wheel and change some old worn-out patterns in my life.*

I arrived home at 5:15am, jumped into my cozy bed and slept soundly for hours with no need to count sheep...or hamsters! I sleepily pondered changing direction in my life, and then I rolled over for a few more hours of sleep.

Changing direction

Women are doing amazing things because we have never had this opportunity before. In the year 2000, I did the Artist's Way exercises with three good friends for a year and we all launched our own businesses. Julia Cameron's exercises were so helpful. We met once a month for a year and did the 12 chapters of the book together, used our creativity, and discovered what we are here for—with the support of each other. We began to see our whole life as an art project.

I planned my next move—my escape—for one year. I decided not to stay in a corporation where they could renege on a prize and then possibly lay you off at any time. I created a new company called Elite Resorts & Spas and decided I would represent some of the best resorts in the U.S.; resorts such as Carneros Resort in Napa, Montage Resort, Surf and Sand in Laguna Beach, Carmel Valley Ranch; even a Luxury Ranch in Montana signed up with me because I had an excellent database of meeting planners who booked group business. I phoned resorts like Ojai

Valley Inn or Royal Palms Resort and asked if they would be interested in retaining an independent sales rep. (I recall the day I first called Sundance Resort; I was so scared. To my surprise, they were interested and said yes. Believe it or not, they were my clients for 17 years.) I charged a monthly retainer and just needed eight resorts to leave my corporate job. I called on companies like Mattel and Honda, and made appointments to go into their offices and meet with their conference, meeting, and event planners with my beautiful iPad presentation. I asked if they would consider having meetings at any of these resorts, saying, "If you want a meeting at Laguna Beach, call me." I received a nice retainer from the main company I was with and got their permission to get contracts with other hotel entities. I had a sticky note on my computer that said, "I signed up eight elite resorts by October 2000," and on October 31, 2000, I signed my eighth resort. I could finally leave the big corporation. They asked me to come back full time, but I said "No, I'm going to be independent now." Ironically, in divine order, 18 years later, that prior company bought my database.

Starting up my new company took a lot of sweat, diligence, and glorious effort. I worked like an energizer bunny in my home office, made sales calls throughout Southern California, and did road shows until one day my adrenals were so flattened out, I was beyond exhausted, and just had no more energy. I went to Miraval Resort, a new destination spa resort in Tucson, and did morning hikes in the desert, learned a new meditation technique, took mindful eating classes etc., got massages, and was power rejuvenated. I realized spas were a wonderful, timely new trend, especially for work-aholics and I decided to focus on representing resorts that had full-service spas.

Action step

Career Clarity - Perfect job exercise:

In the 1980's, I was working at a mind-numbingly tedious job and would hallucinate with boredom as I stapled stacks of papers together for a home developer in Upland, California. I developed a career clarity/job hunting technique where you could write out the ingredients of your perfect job and suspend judgment while you're writing it. The job doesn't need to already exist, but the goal of this exercise is to get you in touch with who you are today. What would the *ingredients* of your perfect job be? On a yellow legal pad, I wrote out all the ingredients of my perfect job. Within one month, I had a wonderful, new job including a new car and everything else on that list. Since the 1980's I have added more features to this powerful exercise and have been sharing it with others in my Reinvent Yourself workshops. Over the past thirty years, I would tweak my perfect job about every three years and add new ingredients, like "using my public speaking ability, helping the environment, using my writing skills, travel to Rio de Janeiro or Thailand," or I'd modify my current job. You are not just re-formatting a resume; you're adding a new dimension to your job. This can prevent you from retiring earlier than you should because you are disgruntled. You might not need to leave your current job; maybe you can just work less hours, modify it, refine it, or tweak it.

This perfect job/next act exercise I've developed is a six-page exercise that I teach in my Reinvent Yourself workshops. This life-changing exercise gets you in touch with who you are today and what you truly desire for your perfect job. In this exercise, you write the ingredients of your perfect job. The job doesn't need to already exist; you are creating it as you write out the ingredients. I've taught this exercise one-on-one and, in many workshops, and it really works. You truly can create your perfect job. You are the only person with your spirit, your personality, and your unique set of talents. This is almost magical. It draws the job to you, instead of sending resumes for the same old job like you've been doing, you are creating a job for the person you are *today*. It's an extremely powerful exercise and it's been proven over and over again that it works, by the many testimonials I receive by email, personal conversations, and voicemails. The more energy, intention, and enthusiasm you put into doing the exercise, the quicker it works. There truly is power in the pen.

Career Clarity - Perfect Job exercise

(Here is a summary of the Perfect Job exercise, which I cover in much more detail through one-on-one coaching and in my workshop.)

Success inventory—take an inventory of the successes, skills, and achievements in your life. This list should remind you of how awesome you are (i.e. school, degrees, work, family, church, volunteering, promotions, titles, happy marriage, raising a family, public speaking, career, achievements etc.).

Write out the ingredients of your perfect job (i.e. salary/income, medical benefits, type of company or boss, enthusiasm for product, location, vacation time, ideal office environment, local/domestic/international travel, using your creativity, opportunity for growth and advancement). Job uses your experience in (list your talents and strengths here—i.e. I use my organizational skills, creativity, computer skills, writing ability, people skills, etc.)

Now, be a little crazy—list some things here you'd almost *pay* to do.

Higher purpose—write out whatever legacy you'd like to leave.

Visualization—write out how you see yourself on your ideal work day; what are you wearing, who are you meeting with, what are you doing? Put excitement into it.

Affirmation: I bless my current position with love and I now accept a wonderful new job or career where I'm richly rewarded, creatively, spiritually, and financially. This is now happening for the highest good of all concerned.

Action step

Write out action steps to help make this happen (i.e. network, internet research, apply to jobs online, call new contacts, invite key contacts out for coffee for field research, update your LinkedIn profile etc.)

When you're two-thirds of your way through life, you realize your time comes *now* or not at all. At this stage of your life, what kind of connections, experiences, and people would you like to meet? How do you grow or shift your business and professional life?

How do you transition to retirement or semi-retirement? Shifts you'd like to make personally? Philanthropy, volunteer work? How do you envision your next act?

Some key things to remember:

Life will be easier when you're doing the thing you really want to do. Get into alignment with what you want. When you're happy, the byproduct is success. Tap into your innovation. Be in the flow and forget what people will think about you. Fall in love with not knowing, and then you have room to learn new things. Fall in love with this moment. You can't get to your purpose through thinking. Ask yourself what life wants from you. What does the bigger part of you want?

Living from the heart is the real secret to success. It takes courage to live from the heart. The mind should serve the heart. When your heart is open, you'll experience flow—more synchronicity. Great leaders speak from their heart. The *why* doesn't get attached to the method. You want to get to a place where you *have* to do it. Meditate, let go, play. Maybe you're here to do something huge. What's your *why*, your vision—why are you doing it? Ask yourself what idea expands you. What idea contracts you? Let go of "I have to..."

The higher alignment of the person—the more you want to help. Find your truth first and create your career or philanthropic work after that.

How do you thrive in the midst of transition? Through reflection, dialogue, and discernment...keep challenging yourself and raising your personal bar. Keep discerning what you intend to say with your life. "This is who I am, and this is what I stand for in the great flow of life."

Action step

Your specific soul lessons

Have you ever said, "Ugh! I just attracted the same old boss, different job!"

It's important to acknowledge how much wisdom you've already gained through life's ups and downs. Is there a dynamic that keeps repeatedly showing up in your life? Do you keep attracting the same type of boss, spouse/partner, co-workers? What was your part in creating this dynamic? Some people keep attracting negative, controlling, competitive bosses or spouses. Maybe it's time to wake up and take note of this pattern. If the only common ingredient in all these scenarios is you, maybe it's time to reflect on your part in subconsciously creating this. How can you change and show up differently?

What does your soul want *more* of? What does your soul want *less* of?

Are you retired, still working full time, or part time? Write the answers to these questions:

As I look back and experience my life, what specific scenes, situations, and behaviors seem to recur?

Are you aware of the same experiences and your reactions to their repetition?

Are the major characters in your life cut from the same cloth? Identify repeating themes or scenarios.

Years from now, as you review your life, what will you regret *not* having done?

If my life was a book and I was the author, what story would I want to tell?

Why not start doing that—writing a new story—now?

Link forward momentum with a cause. If you have a product that changes lives and you don't get it out there, you're stealing from those who need it most.

Take more risks. Lighten up. Ask, *Who am I without my work?*

What were your dreams when you were young?

If I *did* matter, what would I do every day? Live the moment more.

Consider each day you haven't laughed, played, and celebrated your life to be wasted.

"Impossible dreams are possible if you are willing to become the person your dream calls you to be. No dream is ever too big—you just need to become the person it challenges you to be" (Aleta St. James).

Get up earlier. Meditate every single day—that's a non-negotiable—do green juicing, workout, exercise, be aware of diet and nutrition, work, plan date-night time for *love*. Have a beacon you're driving for. Fall in love with the moment and experience the future now. Once you s*ee your vision, just reverse-engineer it.*

Chapter Eight

The Wow Comeback:
Learning to Love the Void

Sometimes you *know* where you want to be; you're chomping at the bit, but you feel like you're wading through quicksand. Simone is a talented, creative young woman who is frustrated and trying to make peace with the stage I call the fertile, friggin' void. She has a bachelor's degree in Communication Studies, is adept at marketing, creative writing, and social media, but is stuck in a catch-22 situation of needing experience to *get* experience. She is working in customer service, handling mundane chores, phone orders, and data entry. Her company's marketing department truly needs her talents, but its overwhelmed marketing manager is insecure, unable, *and* unwilling to delegate those chores. Simone feels like a budding butterfly in the cocoon, ready to emerge and spread her wings; so eager to prove herself and use her talents, but the company is dragging its feet.

What if you're *not* feeling passionate, excited, or motivated? You could be in the neutral zone or in the void. It's so uncomfortable and frustrating, but much good comes out of it. If you rush that stage, you might make a mess and accept something that is not right for you.

Have you ever felt like you're stuck in second gear? You could be in the void. The void is that in-between zone where, on the surface, it seems like nothing is happening, but the void is actually a very fertile place to be. Sometimes on the surface, it seems like nothing is happening, but the void is actually a very fertile place to be. When I'm on my way from point-A to point-C and I'm in process—in the middle, at point-B—it's easy to get frustrated, impatient, make a childish remark, stamp my feet, and say, "But God, I've been praying for this desire for so long. When is it *ever* coming to me?"

Sometimes life forces us to be still and get quiet. A couple years ago, I got a bad case of food poisoning from some salad and it laid me up for five or six days. I was so nauseated that all I could do was lie on my couch, eat clear, watery soup, and drink mint tea. It was a very humbling and depressing week, but it forced me to take some much-needed time to reflect on my life.

I realized I was coming to the end of an 18-year chapter of running my own successful business, Elite Resorts & Spas. It had been a really good run. I represented some of the best resorts on the west coast of the U.S. and I wistfully knew it was coming to a close. Feelings of emptiness, fear of the future, depleted energy, and a void; like, what's next? This business I'd created was my baby, but now with tears streaming down my face, I cried and realized sadly, I'm getting ready to move on.

A surprising gift came to me that same day. I got up from the couch and walked out my front door to get the mail. On my way back in, I noticed once again a small orange pod hanging on my front door. A few days prior, I had almost pulled it off the front door but realized it was the pupa or chrysalis of a butterfly. It had been hanging on my front door for about 10 days. It may have looked like nothing was going on, but big changes were happening inside. Special cells present in the larva were growing rapidly. They were becoming the legs, wings, eyes, and other parts of an adult butterfly. By the fifth day of the food poisoning, I was finally feeling a little better, rising from the couch with a desire to get out into the fresh air. That happened to be the first day of spring, March 21st, a very special day that combined the equinox, an eclipse, and a mega moon. Astrological reports said a major shift took place on the planet that day.

I opened my front door, and low and behold, a beautiful monarch butterfly was emerging out of the orange chrysalis. It shed its skin and what a miracle! A butterfly so delicate, with an orange and black pattern slowly worked its way out of the now translucent pod. It then flew away before my very eyes. It would live two to five months while it mates and lays eggs. Wow, re-birth!

As I was emerging from my own chrysalis, it seemed like such a metaphor for my life. I had gone within to reflect upon this time of transition. I was then ready and excited for the next stage of my own evolution...my encore career...semi-retirement; I wasn't ready to jump straight into retirement.

I knew the old, energizer bunny, frenetic go-getter in me had matured into a more mellow, hopefully wiser woman. I was more accepting and peaceful about my next stage of life and it was exciting. I had learned to trust the still, small voice within. The vision for my next stage was becoming clearer.

As a person who was always into do-do-do, I started to realize it's okay to just *be* and not totally know what's coming next. Yes, it's okay to not know, to be in the in-between stage, full of possibility; it's not an empty place at all.

I read some self-help books and reflected on passions I'd never acted upon before. I connected to them on a deeper, spiritual level. I surprisingly found myself smiling for no special reason. In my mid-sixties, I noticed that my thoughts are more profound, more interesting, and I wouldn't want to trade them for the traumas of being 20 or 30 years old again. Stimulating creativity is good for us when we're in the neutral zone. I wrote new ideas in my journal. This period reignited some hobbies, causes, and my passion to make a difference in the world, to become more fulfilled. I intend to aim as high as I can and shine my light even brighter. It's a transformative time. I truly feel this *is* my most awesome chapter ever. The timing is perfect to spread my wings and soar.

Are you feeling in-between, stuck in the middle, in the void where nothing seems to be jelling or coming together? It's ok! A good friend of mine once said, "I'm on the verge of something big but I'm sick of being on the friggin' verge. I want to verge already!"

Like a butterfly, are you in the chrysalis or pupal stage? Are you like the caterpillar who has yet to transform into a butterfly? Realize that several things are happening and it's not a resting stage. The caterpillar's old body dies and a new body with beautiful wings appears after two weeks.

Maybe the next time nothing seems to be working, you can take a deep breath and ask yourself if you're in the chrysalis. What wonderful transformation could be happening inside you right now? Chrysalis-emergence as a transformed butterfly is indeed one of the wonders of nature. Imagine a butterfly breaking free of the pupae, expanding and drying its wings, and then flying.

If nature can be so magnificent for butterflies, can't I trust that with patience, prayer, meditation, going within spiritually, maybe I will emerge from this period of change transformed and ready to fly? If the butterfly is in its cocoon, it's not *in the pits*, it's preparing and developing; it's not a wasting period. Why would we be any less than a butterfly? Find the blessing in what you're going through before you move on from it. Love the period of the void—infinite, unlimited possibility—before you kiss it goodbye.

If you're in the neutral zone, the void, go deeper and ask, "What is the blessing in this? What's good about this? What am I learning here? What is emerging?" Change the way you look at the situation and realize various key factors are still coming together. The universe is weaving its tapestry and you just can't rush things. Go within, meditate, and get peaceful with what is. Be okay with being in-process and allow the good to unfold in divine timing.

What are some of the ways you can evoke the miracles, increase resilience, rally on a daily basis, and bounce back from any self-doubt to push forward into the new wow life you desire?

I was told by a Vedic astrologer that this life would be fulfillment of the dharma of all my lifetimes. Your wow years can truly be from age 50 onward, and your *biggest* wows can be yet to come. Think bigger, even when you have setbacks. When you do the conscious work, you don't have to age, you can sage—become a person who has wisdom and insight. Get out of your way and keep proactively creating your future

One way to keep proactively creating is to tap into the energy and enjoyment you have felt in some of your key life wow moments. Making a list produces a desire to create even more moments.

Some of my biggest wow moments were:

1. Trips to Yosemite with my family in the big Oldsmobile station wagon with six of my eight brothers and sisters, laughing and joking, hiking up the rocks in the Merced River, staring at the blanket of stars at night, gazing in awe at Yosemite Falls from the Ahwahnee Hotel with my dad. Such a magical moment!

2. The backpacking trip to Europe with my sister and two best friends; laughing our way through the continent at the ages of 20 and 21, then living in London, working in Chelsea, and sharing a flat with my English roommate who was Rod Stewart's former girlfriend.

3. Falling in love with my first boyfriend, Charlie, at the age of 16, then falling in love a few more times in my twenties, thirties, and forties.

4. Moving to a ranch with my ex with his two children, our six horses, three dogs, and six cats.

5. My life-changing experience at Miraval Resort, then creating the representation firm of Elite Resorts & Spas, and building it up to 24 resorts at one point. Traveling to 100 four- and five-star resorts. A peak moment was glamping—glamorous camping—at a luxury ranch in Montana.

6. Teaching Reinvent Yourself workshops. A special wow moment was when a woman came up to me after one of them and told me, "God told me to be here today, and now I know why." That was big for me. I'm passionate about sharing empowerment ideas and I believe this is why I'm here on Earth. What a wonderful, wow feeling!

Action step

What are some top wow moments from your life? List ten and then meditate on how they made you *feel*. Making my list of wow moments really gave me more clarity on the circuitous route my life has taken. Like a river that curves, twists, and meanders, ultimately directing me closer and closer to my life's purpose, I realized each time I took a chance, stuck my neck out, had a heartbreak or setback, changed course, and overcame my fears, I was stronger and closer to my goal. One of my favorite sayings is, "What you want, wants *you*!" What is your story so far? You've heard the saying that "eventually you wear fate down," and that has been true for me. After you write your wow moments, can you see any aha's or common threads? Has your path led you in any special direction? Self-reflection is huge at this time. How can you fill the spaces of your life with actions that wow you and feel like other wow times?

Here are some thought-provoking questions to answer to spark some new ideas.

What makes you uniquely you?

Where do you need to grow? Reverend Michael Beckwith from Agape International Spiritual Center in Beverly Hills says to ask, "What is my growing edge?"

What are some of your earlier achievements?

We did a success inventory in chapter seven, so you can look back on your notes and focus, even if it is all the way back in third grade. I won a spelling bee, I got voted most talented in eighth grade, etc. This exercise is really good for your soul.

What is one of your major fears? Originally one of my major fears was speaking up and accidentally upsetting someone or hurting their feelings. I've learned that it's not necessarily what you say, but *how* you say it. I've had to work on connecting with my heart and learning how to lovingly express myself.

Ponder. Is that fear a fact? Or is it drama that you invented? Through practice and counseling, I have learned to speak up more diplomatically and this fear in me has lessened.

Ponder. Sometimes what appears to be a problem is actually an answered prayer in disguise. It is nourishment—compost—for richer crops. I often think the hardest thing for us to do is what we *came* here to do. Like I mentioned earlier, for me, that was learning to speak up and finding my voice. How about taking some time to ponder and wander? A change of geography can give you a new perspective on your life. One day, when I was feeling stuck, I drove up to Santa Barbara and got a fresh, new perspective on my life. I love the idea of pondering, taking a drive, and ruminating as I look out at the ocean or open spaces, and allowing ideas to come to me instead of just working, slogging away, and striving all the time. Ask yourself a question and take a drive or a walk in nature. Ponder the question as you walk or drive down beautiful roads. Be open to unexpected messages and answers that come to you.

How might an old decision or set of decisions have prepared you for this moment?

Doing action items you're afraid of increases your confidence and helps you bounce back.

Below, brainstorm some ideas of how you could move through your fear and take action.

What are three bold, brave, new things I can do this week to pursue my desires?

Step outside your routine. Think beyond what you'd normally do. Think *bigger*.

Reflect and research what others have done to get inspired and see things in a new light.

This is another Abraham-Hicks technique I do every few weeks, usually on a Saturday morning. I works like magic and I love checking things off, especially on the right side of this list, once they come to pass.

God and the universe's to-do list

This exercise helps you be brave and bold. It's like laying out your big questions on an altar and then releasing them to the universe. Draw a "T" on a blank page. Above the left side of the "T" write "My to-do list" and on the right side of the "T" put "God's to-do list or The Universe's to-do list"—whatever feels right for you. On the left side, write "Things I'm ready to do." These would be simple things like wash the car, get groceries, answer emails, clean the house, etc. On the right side you write big concept things, issues that scare you, or goals you do not have answers for yet, like: help me find my perfect job; help me attract my ideal mate; guide me to the perfect steps for my next career;

orchestrate the perfect, affordable flights for my trip; help me find the perfect, affordable tires for my car, etc.

Use the words that are perfect and ideal in the God and the universe side; this starts your prefrontal cortex working. You put it on an altar and it goes into the quantum field.

I go back three weeks later and just delight in checking off the stuff that happens. It is very powerful.

What is a so-called failure or set-back in your life that you can view differently?

The key to living your wow years to the fullest is to get into that high-vibrational state and stay there. The tools I've listed to pivot, rebound, course-correct, reinvent yourself in chapter two can really help. You can also change your body chemistry with neuro-linguistic programming exercises, and even doing power poses like the super hero or Wonder Woman pose. Harvard professor, Amy Cuddy talks about this in her famous TED Talk, "People are at first embarrassed to try these high-energy poses, but do it and feel fabulous!"

I teach students in my workshops to do the super hero pose before job interviews, and I receive so many testimonials from people, saying they got the job or the sale after they did this pose. I do the Wonder Woman pose before important meetings and it really does work. It brings up your energy and people react positively to your high energy.

Another great way to stay high-vibe and release stress is to breathe deeply. Most of us are actually shallow breathers and we have to remind ourselves to breathe deeply during the day. (I have a sticky note on my computer to remind me to *breathe deeply*.)

I drive quite a bit in Los Angeles and I'll often flip around to various radio stations before I find something I can relate to. At times I enjoy talk radio; however, much of today's radio is polarizing and it just makes you more frustrated and discouraged about the world. Imagine tuning into a radio station where *the life you really want is already in progress.* It's already unfolding if you can *trust the work.* Well, 99% of your creation *is* already in progress. It is the result of the energy, thoughts, and sparks of desire you've already launched in the past. Now is the time to release attachment to the outcomes.

How many of your estimated 70,000-plus thoughts a day are negative and repetitive? If your inner radio station has been playing old, worn-out, negative thoughts over and over again, it's time to tune into your own, new high-vibe radio station. Change the station. Consciously choose exciting, enthusiastic, bold, new thoughts. Make a decision to align with a new higher-frequency radio station called My Ideal Life Radio Station. This radio station is now coming through loud and clear with a great life that's *already in progress.* Tune in. Release any resistance. Imagine—if you're looking for love, wow, my man is already here. How does it feel? Thank you; it's already done. In 1900, Max Planck discovered there was a direct relationship between a photon's frequency and its energy. The higher the frequency of light, the higher the energy.

What is the energy corresponding to the frequency of *your* favorite radio station?

Is it low-frequency anger, fear, or prejudice, or is it broadcasting solution-based, loving, enthusiastic, high-vibrational new ideas? Positive, inspirational, stimulating messages?

Frequencies beyond man's attention range like x-rays and radio waves are hidden from view—all the more powerful, all the more intelligence within a given space. Higher earth frequencies are allowing people on the planet with higher frequencies activated in their system to expand even more in consciousness.

It's time to clear all past issues, forgiving yourself and others. Open your mindset to the universal level; help yourself to receive your full power. Clear blockages, release old negative patterns, past issues at the cellular level, and replenish with new, vibrant higher frequency energies that bring clarity and focus. Open your heart to more love, joy, passion, prosperity, and enthusiasm to live life at your fullest potential.

Listen and start living your dream.

Action step

What name would you like to call your new radio station? High-vibe Radio?

Write about your ideal life and imagine it is now in progress. Close your eyes. Think about it. Feel it. How does it *feel*? Smile. Get into that excited feeling state and rehearse how thrilled you are that your ideal job, most awesome chapter of life ever, perfect mate, and dream home are here *now*. Woo-hoo!

For even more impact, record this ideal life scenario into your cell phone using your phone's voice memo feature. I frequently record positive messages in my own voice into my cell phone and then listen to it. It's even more effective to have soft, spa-music playing in the background while you make these recordings into your phone. Try taking a power walk with your ear buds in your ears, listening to your custom-designed voice memos—your own high-vibe radio station!

"Dream as if you'll live forever. Live as if you'll die today" (James Dean, Actor).

What if you gave up on your dream just one day before your miracle occurred? One step before your goal was ready to manifest? One day before your ideal mate, your dream man, or woman appeared? If you believe and are persistent in following your dream, you eventually *do* wear fate down.

"Don't give up before your miracle happens" (Fannie Flagg).

"The breakdown in your business or personal life is leading to the breakthrough. The breakthroughs always happen" (Max Wellspring).

Believe it. Even if it's five minutes, five days, five years before the miracle occurs. Don't give up. Believe. How many people think they're not pretty enough, remarkable, or good enough? They need talent, belief, and resilience. Talent speaks for itself. Whatever talent you have—singing, dancing, painting, repairing things, designing, drawing, building, carpentry, writing, photography, planning creative events, playing sports, cooking, baking, nurturing children, etc. *believe* in yourself.

What if you hadn't stepped up and spoken to some key person who became your publisher, your client, your spouse? *Be brave, be bold.* Say, "People are going to love (me, my book etc.). They just don't know it yet."

Chapter Nine

What is Your Wow?

My 60-year-old friend, Colleen, has reinvented herself several times in the past 40 years. She had a full career for 30 years as a sales and training director for a high-end skincare product. After two marriages, becoming a widow, and several moves, Colleen went back to college and got her associates degree at the age of 58. She also had a background in singing, acting, and theatre, so she thought, "I might as well do something I enjoy!" She has stories to tell and wants to make a difference in the world through screenwriting, film, or moving pictures, either on the big screen or on people's phones. She wants to make content that reaches people's hearts through film. She was previously afraid, but overcame her doubts and fears and applied to USC's excellent film school. She was accepted there with scholarships, grant money, and student loans, which covered the annual $72,000 tuition. Colleen said the intuitive message she got was, "It's not your money, it's mine. Your ability to earn that is a gift from God and the universe." Majoring in Theatre Arts, with a minor in Cinematic Arts and Screenwriting has been the most amazing experience for her. She still has doubts and then is surprised when she gets an A-. May 2020 is her graduation date. She says, "Wow! I'm a woman with 2020 vision!" She keeps following her spirit, wherever it leads. This quote is her guiding light: "Happiness is when what you say, what you think, and what you do are in harmony" (Gandhi). She believes that since she's been true to herself and in alignment with body, mind, and spirit, life is miraculous. She has to pinch herself as she strolls through the beautiful USC campus with its sculptures, gardens, flowers, and fountains, marveling, "Wow! I co-created this with my spirit!"

I led a workshop in Santa Barbara at Casa de Maria Retreat a few years ago called Act 3: How to make this your most awesome chapter ever; the attendees were all in their sixties. One of the women was going through a divorce. After 30 years of marriage, she was excited and afraid to finally be defining and designing her own life. Her husband had constantly criticized her and his presence in her life had drained her. She was starting to fulfill some lifetime dreams and she realized she had to be on her own to do this. Her energy was completely different now without him in her life. She was researching new classes and courses that interested her at this stage in her life. She was scared but full of eager anticipation. In your wow years, you have the opportunity to look at service, your calling, and your purpose in the world. I will direct you through a series of questions that will bring you to a deeper consciousness in all three areas, but first we need to prepare who you are going to essentially *be* in this most important act of your life?

If you don't examine your life purpose now, when *will* you do it? It's now or never.

First, we have the power to take the fear out of aging. We can actually get excited about it, flip the fear, and embrace the next chapter. The mother of my friend, Janet, looked shriveled and old and was an invalid in a rest home at 63 years old. She had basically been a hypochondriac in a nursing home for years. As the daughter of this woman, Janet vowed to live her life differently. She successfully raised three children, and at 63 years old, she is vibrant, has a viable job, is hip, attractive, and youthful.

Here are some key act-three preparation questions to ask yourself:

How will you spend the rest of whatever time you *do* get?

Will you quit your job?

Who are you without your work, anyway?

Should you work part time or fully retire?

If you have a partner, how does your spouse or partner feel about retiring?

Have you discussed a retirement timeframe with your partner?

Should you downsize? Where will you live?

How much will you travel?

How much time will you spend with family?

Old dreams can be updated and new ones revealed. It's scary! Why do we fear change and transition so much? You dream of leaving the working world, but what is next? Freedom from work to freedom <u>to</u> work in an encore career? Can you combine service and continued income?

Marc Freedman calls this time of life "<u>The sweet spot</u>—it's an intersection between two dimensions of life—our Indian summer." He says, "Human beings don't realize the height of their capacity until the shadows start getting longer." *The Bonus Years*. Mortality, longevity, and urgency; time is more precious; you really want to make each day count, especially when you see certain friends passing away in their fifties and sixties. You start focusing even more on a healthy lifestyle, hoping to stretch out these bonus years. You're ready to deeply dive into the possibilities, feeling a strong sense of urgency to create a more meaningful experience (within your current archetype, to start). You're all in for new ideas, diving deeply, and getting going on your next chapter.

You want to make a big impact; live and leave a legacy. You're pondering time lived and time left to live; thinking more deeply about purpose beyond yourself.

Father Richard Rhor says, "We're addicted to the status quo and past, even when it's killing us." Change asks us to let go, but we're better at holding on. It's time to take risks and expand, but you may ask these poignant questions:

How can you now serve at an even higher level?

What are you really here to do?

How can you give more to others?

Do you save the world or take time to savor the world?

Why can't you do both? Save *and* savor the world?

It's time to imagine what your life could be life if you were brave enough to do more of what you love. If your life was a book and you were the author, you know how the first two-thirds has been written, but how would you want the rest of the story to unfold? How do you want to write the rest of this book?

My friend, Patti, always had a unique response to aging. She never acted her age in the appropriate, prescribed age group. As a child, she couldn't wait to be older. As a younger person she always aspired to act and live in an older person's era. She got married, raised children, divorced, and then lived in a survival state until the 1980's when she experimented with her first true feelings of freedom. She immersed herself in a younger, California lifestyle of sex, drugs, and rock and roll, dated younger men, and then made a career change from social work to film publicist in mid-life. She then told everyone she knew that she wanted to find a man, found her new man, and remarried. Whether older or younger, Patti never subscribed to the number that corresponded with her actual age. She says, "I don't deal with numbers. Come from your own truth, your own soul...your joy."

Patti also ascribes to the philosophy, "As you get older, you need to cozy up to death." What does that mean? You don't feel or look like you used to and you can't escape the fact that you have limited time. If you've lived a busy life fraught with distraction, it's time to <u>be present...to keep it clear and clean</u>. No time for platitudes. This *is* the most critical time, the most profound time in your life, and you must do whatever it takes to make it the clearest of reality.

Joseph Campbell wrote about *The Hero's Journey*. The hero leaves his ordinary world for the first time and crosses the threshold into adventure. He has setbacks, sometimes causing him to try a new approach or adopt new ideas. Then there's the ordeal— the hero experiences a major hurdle or obstacle, such as a life-or-death crisis. In a decisive crisis, he wins a victory and then comes home changed or transformed. Jane Fonda says, "Our third act is where it all comes together." Here's a new way to look at it and even reframe your life experiences: So far, I've lived an amazing life. My life prepared me perfectly for this next stage— my most awesome chapter ever!

A wonderful Act 3 doesn't just happen by default. You need to start with a life review, get clarity on what you want to do for the next twenty to thirty years, plan your Act 3, write down your goals, visualize, practice gratitude, and commit to a non-negotiable, positive daily ritual to really empower your day and change your life.

Action step

This is a good time to reflect on your life so far; to see your challenges, ups and downs, painful experiences, losses and achievements in perspective. This will help prepare you for your Act 3.

1. Briefly jot down one of your worst, most challenging experiences; one of your biggest regrets. We all have disappointments, regrets, and mistakes we feel we've made. Maybe your first or second chapter of life wasn't what you were expecting.

2. It takes real work to see your failures, heartbreaks, divorce, setbacks, misfortunes, and adversity and perceive them as blessings. Now ask yourself how you can reframe these experiences and embrace these past challenges as a blessing. Science has found that 50% of what we remember isn't even accurate anyway. It's part of a much longer divine plan that I couldn't see when I was in the middle, but it was part of an arc getting me to a much higher place; to a much higher level. Author, Diana Loomans says, "Had I known in the beginning what would happen in the end, I would have prayed for it." In a voice of wisdom, reframe the ending under a story archetype—like a princess or a prince. How did this give me incredible character?

3. Write your Act 3e. Start the sentence with "My Act 3 began..." and write that story now. If I knew life happened *for* us and not *to* us, how would I write my next chapter of life? In planning for the road ahead, imagine your life in a different way. What could my life be like?

Go meet yourself in the future. See yourself in your perfect future. You're 90 years old. How were your last 30 years? Write my Act 3 began...

Example: "My Act 3 began (date). The first two-thirds of my life was very rich and full of so many blessings and lessons. It all started to get even better when I took time for reflection, a quiet weekend, or attended a fabulous transformative retreat. During that time or retreat, I had so many aha's and got such clarity about how the path I took had taught me so many important lessons. I reframed the experiences and saw how the journey was actually perfect for who I had aspired to become. I started to see what I really wanted to do in my Act 3. I wrote down my spiritual, financial, emotional, and career/service goals, and everything unfolded in such divine timing. After that weekend, I met a wonderful man/woman and we fell in love; we experienced the best, most satisfying love relationship of our lives. I volunteered with my local homeless shelter, joined our community theater, wrote my book, developed powerful innovative workshops, became a successful workshop leader, speaker..." or whatever your dreams are now.

We're fortunate to know about raised consciousness in aging; our ancestors didn't have these messages. Celebrate this time in your life. You're older but wiser. What is your niche? Your version of Act 3 can be a totally new paradigm. Play to your strengths, personality, and prior experience. If you're still working full time, part time, or volunteering, here are some questions to consider:

Who would you like to work with?

What specific problem can you solve for others?

Can you create a specific service for a specific market based on your unique expertise? Who can you help the most?

Who do you want to serve?

Make them your niche. Be the go-to person for your niche. Know exactly who it is you want to serve.

Service

What causes are you passionate about? Whether it's homelessness, protecting children, environmental causes, human rights causes, political activism, tutoring students, human trafficking; causes like autism, Alzheimer's, cancer, or Alcoholics Anonymous, you may start feeling a new sense of urgency to make a difference in the world. From my early twenties, I always knew I had a passion to empower others and make a positive difference on environmental issues and animal rights causes. Over the past 30 years, I've volunteered with organizations like Tree People, Heal the Bay, People for the Ethical Treatment of Animals, World Wildlife Fund, ASPCA, and others. Service adds so much meaning to your life. VolunteerMatch (www.volunteermatch.org) is a very effective way to match you up with causes you're passionate about and connect you with local non-profits committed to your cause.

Look at service as a holy connection; going joyfully through the world, seeing the sacred in the great sea of being. You realize there's no part of your life that isn't service. What makes your inner tuning fork hum?

Your calling – *What makes your heart sing*

What is your higher purpose—your reason for getting up in the morning, outside of yourself? Sometimes it takes a crisis to make you push the pause button and reflect. What really matters in life? It's time for courage; to take more risks. Purpose is a choice. Steve Jobs said, "We're here to put a dent in the universe. Otherwise why else even be here?" He will go down in history of business and industry as a legendary figure like Thomas Edison or Henry Ford. Your gifts plus your passions plus your values equals your calling. Get out of your comfort zone and experiment. It takes a lot of experimentation. = *mistakes*

Purpose moment

Living in the right question. Ask yourself what life is asking of you today. Start with where you are now. Act purposely and the theme or purpose will show up. Every moment can be a purpose moment. Are you a giver or a taker in this moment? Your default purpose is to grow and to give. Are you growing and giving? If so, you're on purpose.

Some people think that unless they're growing a grand design, they're not living on purpose, but the core of purpose is compassion. Listen to another person. Give a kind word or a pat on the back. It takes practice. Life is nothing more than purpose moments. Practice compassion, and purpose will naturally follow. It takes practice to be really happy, to find your why and what's your contribution. It's fundamental to our survival.

It's not easy, though. Only one in five people want to get up and go to work every day (Gallup Poll).

We need to acknowledge a new stage around retirement age— *before old age*. We're facing a 30-year vacation we don't necessarily want and possibly can't really afford. Marc Freedman invites us to rethink the whole trajectory of life. It's now a longevity revolution. Do you really want to be doing the same thing for longer? Millions of people are making a monument for what used to be the leftover years. One in four people are entrepreneurial. More people are living with purpose, passion, productivity, service, and social impact; for example, being a creative consultant and half-time working with the homeless.

"The greatest potential for growth and self-realization exists in the second half of life" (Carl Jung).

To help create your Act 3 and serve the greater good, it's time for experimentation, so how about a try-before-you-buy concept through internships, job shadowing, or volunteering through the Peace Corp, Americorp, or Teach for America, etc.?

Due to labor shortages, more internship programs are being created to help us go from midlife to our next act. Internships are being offered later in life, where you can create a new brand, learn new skills, and eventually be hired by the company where you intern. You can bring your skills and even contacts to your new area of expertise. AARP says it's never too late for an internship and they call them return-ships, which are specifically designed internships for people returning to the workplace. (Remember Robert DeNiro in the film, *The Intern?*) Some sharpen their skills in a work environment that may have changed significantly since their last experience as employees. A program called Relaunch offers career reentry programming and works with about 30 large companies in a variety of programs.

Whether it's retirement or making a radical shift to a new profession, I've done it; you can do it too and if you have to *lean* into it, that's okay. Start planning your escape and please keep your pension in mind if you're just two years from retirement.

Action step

Now, you're entering Act 3. How do you bring your job experience to service? Consider the following questions:

What is your calling? How can you now use your work experience to serve others?

How might your work skills bring good to your community and the planet?

How can you leave the world a better place?

What are the needs around you that aren't being fulfilled?

Once you pose a powerful question to the universe, like "What did I come here to do?" watch for the answers to come in fun, synchronistic ways through chance phone calls, bumper stickers, billboards, and even annoying interruptions. Insights and revelations can come through a crazy break in your routine. I was thinking about making a change today and I got an email titled, "Change is in your hands." It made me realize I could send some emails out that would initiate the changes I wanted to make.

I know so many people in my life and I love networking to help others. When I meditate in the morning and am in the flow, I will effortlessly meet the exact people who are supposed to help me or receive my assistance. Sometimes though, I get wrapped up in my own plan, and I see events initially as disruptions, postponements, or detours; I start to get discouraged. I can tell you time and time again, these incidents are actually answered prayers. Somewhere along the line, I had wished for this outcome; it just does not always arrive when or how I expected.

I visited my brother and sister in law in North Carolina for a week and I had been looking forward to the one day left of my Christmas vacation, during which I had planned to dedicate the afternoon to work on this book. I had committed to using some vacation time for this pet project; however, a couple of their friends stopped by that last afternoon and my plans were thwarted. At first, I was disappointed, but then I resolved to accept fate, took a deep breath, and sat politely with them at the kitchen table, having tea on that cold December day, listening to them chat about their lives.

The visiting couple had retired a few years ago to Asheville, South Carolina from California to be near their daughter. They heard it was a charming city with art, culture, beauty, and abundant walking paths. They were about 67 years old—and wouldn't you know it? They had some fascinating input and advice on how to reinvent retirement. They were the perfect couple to interview about the new wave of baby boomer retirees, since they were on the leading edge of the first boomers to retire—they were born in 1945. I took copious notes during our lively discussion and it was a fascinating afternoon. They weren't an interruption; they were an *answered prayer*. They added the perfect firsthand experience I was seeking about retirement. How often do we get frustrated and misinterpret these chance meetings as annoying delays, interruptions, and curves in the road, or detours from our path? If we're too focused on a strict, single-minded route with our blinders on, we can miss the blessing in these serendipitous meetings. *Every meeting is an opportunity!*

On a separate occasion, I waited for hours one night at the Hotel Angeleno in Los Angeles in their penthouse restaurant for a client who was caught in heavy traffic on the 405 Freeway. I chatted with Jason, the restaurant manager, for an hour while I waited patiently for my client. Jason confided in me that he was tired of LA traffic and his real passion was to move to Montana and work there. The next day, I connected him with a luxury ranch resort I was affiliated with north of Missoula, Montana and he actually got a great job there as their food and beverage manager. I was the answer to Jason's prayer that night. His life completely changed after our conversation. He now hunts and fishes and works on a 10,000-acre luxury ranch. By the way, my client never did show up. He called and said the traffic was just way too jammed, so he turned around and went home. I learned that night it wasn't about *me*; it was about Jason. Wow! I was *his* answered prayer. *Be the answer to someones prayer.*

"When we give out, tenfold comes back on the return current" (Patricia Cota Robles). When you feel aliveness around the referral or the suggestion, take action on that. On the other hand, when you feel your heart sink like a clunk, there is probably a better way to go. With Jason, it felt exactly right. Sometimes with others, I may need to take a twenty-four hour pause and ask myself more questions.

Am I trying to force things and push the river, so to speak? Or can I float downstream and allow life to just flow?

Maybe it's okay to just be still in the moment. Sometimes the path of surrender is the answer. When you can't fight and you can't flee, then just *flow*.

Today, I was waiting for answers from about six people and no one was getting back to me. I'm learning to take a deep breath when life doesn't seem to be going my way. I ask, "What's the blessing or gift in this situation?" I took a one-hour break and aired myself out by taking a walk on Manhattan Beach. I released the frustration and just enjoyed the warm, sunny day, passing the time with a little window-shopping. I bumped into a lovely friend, Alice, who told me about a new Pilates class. I've been looking for a new Pilates class, so there you go—another answered prayer. The answers are there and they are being revealed in amazing ways. Next time, I'll try embracing the unexpected.

Action step

What prayers were answered for you today?

Was a delay or an interruption really an answered prayer?

Were *you* someone's answered prayer?

Are you locked into a rut of old, repetitive patterns?

Allow some spontaneity. We've had to learn self-discipline in school and work life, so sometimes it's hard to let go of control in our lives.

Is your life over-planned, rigidly-scheduled and over-calculated?

It's good to have a schedule, but maybe you can let it flow more organically.

How about allowing for some unstructured time?

If you're on electronic overload, how about disconnecting from your electronic devices, even for one day, like a Sunday, for some digital detox? Be present and available to who you really are.

What wants to come forth next?

Are you experiencing a discouraging, frustrating setback or possibly another answered prayer?

Chapter Ten

Re-wirement

How do I make as big an influence as I can while I'm here on the planet?

I worked with a client named Beth, who realized she subconsciously repeated an old pattern with a certain type of boss who lacked integrity. Beth had sold high-end office furniture in Los Angeles for 25 years. She thought she had finally manifested the perfect job, working diligently to reach her sales goals, until she found out her boss tried to cheat her out of her well-earned bonus. She was financially fortunate enough to be able to quit and semi-retire at the age of 63. She did the Perfect Job exercise and decided to learn sustainable gardening and volunteer to teach botanical garden classes in Manhattan Beach. She took their classes in sustainable landscaping with native plants, volunteered, teaching drip irrigation, rain barrels, and garden tool selection all over Los Angeles, and she has now completely reinvented herself as a well-paid part-time master gardener. She enjoys traveling with her husband and loves that she's also making a positive difference for the environment.

I'm now quite a fan of semi-retirement, and it can actually be a form of re-wirement...like rewiring your brain; rewiring your brain means connections between neurons in your brain are changing— changing the way the system works. What is retirement anyway? Should it even *be*? For some people, retirement can actually be re-higher-ment — going higher — where we reboot ourselves and invest in the upgraded version. We get the opportunity to take the fear out of aging and get excited about it. We get to flip the fear.

Staying in the game and semi-retiring is so much more interesting if you commit to working on *your* terms. I asked a retired, older gentleman who took many cruises around the world, "Which cruise-line do you like the best?"

He said, "Royal Caribbean," and I asked, "Why?"

"Oh, they have the best dinner rolls!" *Yikes!* I thought, *if my preferences in retirement ever get reduced to how good the dinner rolls are, please shoot me!*

How do people change after 65, or even 55? Some people start to behave like an old person and believe they are done and cooked. If I hear someone say, "I am old," I do a mudra and flick my hands saying, *Cancel, cancel.* (A mudra is a symbolic hand gesture used in Hindu and Buddhist ceremonies and statuary to tune out bad energy.) My mom was a great example because she was always young at heart. She would do a daily four-mile walk on the beach, listening to tunes on her walk-man when she was 76 years old. I'd say, "Mom, what are you listening to today?" She replied, "Oh, reggae—I quite like that reggae." She was always open to new music.

I had lunch with an old friend who had unfortunately become a grumpy retiree. He shared a litany of complaints and had a scowl on his face as he proceeded to say that nothing was going right in the world. I tried to steer the conversation to more positive topics. His wife's mother was very ill, his back ached, and he complained that the economy was not doing well; the Republicans and Democrats in Congress should all be thrown out of office. The Middle East is in an endless cycle of violence and today's healthcare system made everything even worse. Overall, from his perspective, the world was in a complete mess. He's 74 years old and lost all his joie d vivre—joy of living. All these are truths, but there's also a lot going right in the world. I agreed with him for a while and then tried to shift the conversation to the positive things in his life.

My dad often said that when many people retire, they start to die. I knew a man who had been a successful insurance company executive and had become bored with the insurance industry, so at the young age of 55 years old, he retired with the potential of living another thirty to forty years. He loved to play golf, but that's all he did after retirement and his life had been reduced to hitting a little white ball around various golf courses every day. He would slam his clubs down in anger when something didn't go right and he'd stomp off the golf course if the players in front of him were moving at too slow a pace. So much anger inside and what a temper!

What both of these men had in common was a lack of passion and purpose in their lives. Too many people look forward to retirement without really thinking about *how* they'll fill all those hours in a meaningful way every day. They are missing out on the wow years. The prevalent trend with baby boomers is now semi-retirement and encore careers. Many people want to stay in the game somehow and transfer their skills to more meaningful work at a non-profit, for example. You'll live longer if you stay engaged, healthy and fit, and get excited about gardening, volunteering, coaching a team, helping animals, etc. The definition of retirement is changing. At one time, retirement was about a time to relax and take it easy. Thirty years ago, we worked till age 65, then we statistically died at age 70 to 72. Retirement was a very short period in old age. "The retiree today is younger, healthier, fitter, and sharper. As a result, retirement is about life and living and keeping busy...Younger at heart, busier, and happier doing things on their terms and their schedule" (*The top 5 new retirement trends and how they will affect your retirement*, Jim Yih).

It could be a truth that your current life has become stale or a profession has ended because it needed to. When a job ends, you may struggle to see some divine order at play in your life. Every moment of your life offers a new opportunity to deepen your understanding and see what blessings might be coming. Dawn always follows darkness; trust that everything is actually in divine order.

Action step

Are you looking forward to or fearful of retirement? Maybe a job has ended and you're wondering what to do now. How are you going to remain relevant and also pay your bills? What are some ways you can rewire your brain and open up to change? Write your ideas now.

More people than ever are working in retirement. Work and retirement can definitely coexist. The biggest difference is that they have identified what they love, not what they have to do. People retire from large corporations and go back to continue to do part-time consulting projects. They turn lifetime hobbies into businesses, enjoying a little extra income using their time for what they love. We'll see more and more of these retirees who work in retirement—semi-retirement. Baby boomers may do phased retirement because there won't be enough people to replace the demographic bulge, going from five days a week to three days a week to one day a week to full retirement. Maybe job sharing, but not cold turkey. Money is important, but for true happiness, we need to think differently. Think about life and what it means to you in retirement. Refer back to some of the wow moments questions you answered in chapter nine. How can you apply these questions to rewire instead of retire?

Here's an exercise that will help you be *present* and truly appreciate your wow moments without letting them slip by:

Here is my wow-moments exercise:

Take a deep breath and connect to your heart. Be open to deserving and receiving. Make a path to the universal flow.

1. Think back to four wow moments in your life—real life experiences from your past.

   List one to four wow moments from your life. (Examples: Your first paycheck, getting your driver's license, seeing Yosemite Falls for the first time, your first love, the birth of your child/children, your wedding day, buying your first home, creating your own successful business, being invited to speak at your first industry event, etc.

   I. _BIRTHS   KIDS/G KIDS_

   II. _FIRST   HIKE_   SPEAKERS

   III. _BRIDGES — BERAU ETC - CONNECTING_

   IV. _SPEAKING- D'VAR, UMAA, POEM-HUNA_

2. Connect with the wow's happening in your life now. What are they? What do you have in your life now with which to be wow'ed?

3. Visualize and feel the wows that are coming. Be open and receptive to your wows that are on their way to you. What are your wows yet to come?

4. Feel free to continue to share your wows via email, as they come into your life, on my Facebook page (www.facebook.com/Your-Wow-Years) or on Instagram (www.instagram.com/yourwowyears/).

Practice rewiring your brain

The latest research in neuroscience and psychology on neuroplasticity shows that rewiring your brain can improve virtually every aspect of your life. Here's a brief summary of *Five Ways to Rewire Your Brain for Meaningful Life Changes* by Dr. Hilary Stokes

1. Identify the beliefs that support your intention
2. Embrace your positive emotions
3. Visualize
4. Take actions that support your intention
5. Repeat, repeat, repeat—use it or lose it. Retirement years have gone from 20 years of a person's life to 25 to 30 years due to increased life expectancy. In 1900, life expectancy was 47 years; today, it's 78 years. In 1900, one in a million could live to be 100; now it's one in ten thousand. We are living an average of 34 years longer than our great grandparents did. Surveys reveal that seven out of 10 baby boomers expect to be working in their retirement years. Volunteering, making a difference, new adult retirement communities, i.e. three women purchasing a house together at the ages of 57, 62, and 64. Retirees are boating, hiking, biking, moving downtown, giving up their car, and moving to milder temperatures. Perpetual employment has become the *norm* and it helps maintain a comfortable lifestyle.

One of my role models is Jane Fonda, still vital and engaged at the age of 80. She says of the ages of 60 years old and onward, "Act 3 of life is a vital, integrated part of our overall story; the potential-filled culmination of the first two acts." Robert Redford is 81 and just starred in multiple films the past few years. There are so many options, so which one is right for me? Your personality doesn't change if you've been running 80 mph; you need to prepare emotionally too. I want to look and feel like Jane Fonda on the outside and on the inside. Stay relevant. Be around different ages; work hard, play hard.

I've been speaking to men and women lately who are recently retired, and they've been sharing their insights about retirement. My 68-year-old retired friend, Pepper, is loving this time in his life. He enjoys having wide-ranging knowledge, far reaching experience, accumulated wisdom, and a more robust sense of humor when interacting with people. He finds that he's more willing to relax and look back on his foibles, not the least bit ashamed to expose his vulnerabilities and laugh at them at the same time. He loves having time to reflect on that most valuable commodity of all—a broader perspective of life experiences—as he gets a little bit older.

Challenges of retiring too early

Retirement can be too soon if you haven't saved enough money. It could be more practical to be semi-retired. Often people fool themselves and retire before the money is sufficient. You don't want to retire until the money is correct. A friend of mine quit his job at UCLA in order to follow his passion as an inventor for a product in snowboarding. He immediately racked up $40K in debt. He said, "Just a warning, Rita; don't quit the day job too soon." I really learned from him. He struggled for a long time. That was why I spent my final year at my corporate job, saving money, planning my escape, and leaning into my new career. It's a great idea to meet with a financial planner who can help you map out your next 20 to 30 years.

A couple years ago, I was playing golf in Palm Springs and I was paired with a retiree who mentioned to me that he couldn't turn on the heat in the winter or water his lawn because he was on a fixed income and it would cost him $30-$50 more a month. I thought, *that will never be me!* For one thing, I hate being cold. It was a warning to me to save enough money for retirement. It may be time to meet with a good financial planner to navigate your finances in your next chapter. This is a helpful website with good cost-saving tips for retirees: www.aarp.org.

Not everybody is made for retirement. My friend, Linda, does not like to do "fluff" activities. She always wants to be doing stimulating, meaningful work that has a bearing on the world around her. If that requires labor, she would rather be doing that than hitting a golf ball around.

Action step

How will you fill your retirement time with meaningful work, play, and still be of service? Write your ideas now.

A man of about 67 said that since retiring, he has had a challenge handling his thoughts and opinions about the past in a positive way. It took him a while to get over being defined by his work. He tries to stay up on all the technological changes, but he says it's like he woke up recently and it seems like the world has changed from under him.

He was pleasantly surprised to notice a lot of his retired friends had gone back to revisit an early dream they had during the ages of 18 to 35, before they were raising a family; ideas that were on the back burner, like writing a novel or a song, taking up painting, etc.

I like to reframe my past instead of judging myself as not good enough. Reframe it and say, *Now is the perfect time for me to manifest these dreams, and my past experiences have fully prepared me for who I am today; after all, they brought me here.* If you remain open to learning, you can change the redundancy of that old familiar cycle of constantly beating yourself up. Get beyond your analytical mind. Close your eyes and mentally start rehearsing the new feelings you want. Your brain is a record of the past and it can now become a map to the future. Decide to *change*. *Act* like a happy, enthusiastic, positive, joyful person. Feel what the future will feel like ahead of the experience. Make a different choice. Respond to those old, judgmental thoughts differently. Become a creator of your world. Take a deep breath and say, "I'm willing to change. This is the perfect age for me to step into this new paradigm. I'm now feeling worthy, lovable, talented and successful."

A piece of advice—be especially proactive about your health, and if at all possible, stay out of the hospital. Three most important things people aspire to are health, wealth, and happiness. You can't enjoy wealth and happiness without health. This is a great time to study up on healthy eating, exercise, well-being, and balance. Do stretching exercises every day. "As a general goal, aim for at least 30 minutes of moderate physical activity every day. If you want to lose weight, maintain weight loss, or meet specific fitness goals, you may need to exercise more" (Mayo Clinic).

My vibrant, healthy friend, Kathi, has some excellent thoughts on aging well. Here are her favorite tips:

- Don't let an old person move into your body; don't let a sick person move into your body;

- Move: stretch, walk, stand on your tiptoes, balance on one leg and then the other;

- Lift weights, walk while you talk—both on the phone and while chatting with a friend in your home; go out for a walk as you catch up;

- Speak uplifting, happy thoughts and never run yourself down or make deprecating comments about yourself; The vast majority of ill people are sick primarily because they aren't happy.

- Do not make comments about how old you are followed by musing about 'when I'm in an old folks' home' or 'when I'm being pushed around in my wheelchair...' Always envision yourself as youthful of body, mind, and spirit, and healthy until the end. LONG TERM CARE

- Wake up each morning grateful to be alive and healthy;

- Live with passion. Do not write yourself off as through because of your age.

- Fill your mind with possibility thoughts every day.
- Have friends and keep in touch with them; keep in close contact with family;
- Have interests and adventures outside of family ones, i.e. don't be insular with family gatherings to the exclusion of spending time with friends;
- Good nutrition is vital. Eliminate most of the processed foods and artificial ingredients from your diet if possible. Posture is critical. Many (most) old people get stoop-shouldered, and in the process, lose height. While it's not critical that we maintain our original adult height, I think it is a real shame that we become so stooped as we age. Lifting weights and focusing on posture or doing yoga and planks can really be effective in keeping our spines strong. The dowager's hump is a definite sign of age and robs us of our bodily elegance.

Norman Vincent Peale says, "Think joy, talk joy, practice joy, share joy, saturate your mind with joy, and you will have the time of your life all your life. And what's more, you will stay alive as long as you live."

Who knows? Maybe we'll be pioneers in never-tirement. I always want to be fully engaged as a lifelong learner. Hey, baby boomers! Celebrate. This *is* what the new version of 60-plus looks like, and we look pretty darn good! I know this is going to be my most awesome stage of life yet. I'm even envisioning a time where young women can't wait to be in their sizzling sixties. Let's put some wow into our now. Bring it on!

Action step

What do I now want out of life? Am I inclined to be a never-tiree? How can I put some more *wow* into now and the coming years?

Let's change the next generation and be a model for those who are retiring. Tell yourself, "I love you." Ask yourself, "Is there anything special I can do for you today?" What do you really want to do? Take yourself on an outing; fix your hair in a new style. Appreciate yourself; tell yourself you're beautiful. Love you; tell yourself what your good qualities are. Forgive yourself for any judgment you've been holding against yourself. If you've felt you didn't get it right, keep trying. Release the judgment. Do something new today. Do something brave; something bold. You're as old as you feel. What is a day? What is a year? The real age is the age your heart feels. If you feel young, you *are* young.

"And in the end, it's not the years in your life that count; it's the life in your years" (Abraham Lincoln). Our most timeless president.

Marci Alboher created Encore.org and he offers a Purpose Prize to those who do that best. You can read amazing stories of people who used their old job skills to create unique, new programs to help others. Where do you get started on this new path? You can try volunteering, internships, experimenting, and job shadowing. A former food distributer who volunteered with VISTA at the San Francisco Food Bank noticed that all donations were canned goods. He used his contacts in the produce industry and now 120 million pounds of produce are being donated yearly to the San Francisco Food Bank.

Boomers had more advantages, more freedom, not conventional marriages, etc., so we're primed to not have a conventional retirement. Our generation of retirees is so unique because we have had exposure to more information, we are more vibrant, more healthy, and younger looking; most of us don't want to (*and* due to economic factors *can't afford* to) fully retire.

There is a unique opportunity to innovate and offer new solutions to this new growing segment of would-be retirees. We're scratching our heads, saying, "Hmmmm…what's next?" For me, it isn't taking cruises every year with a spouse, playing golf, and retiring to Leisure World. There must be a happy medium somewhere, and my intention is to share with others tools to use their work and life experience combined with passion and purpose to supplement their income, give more to others, and add more meaning to life.

Action step

How might your work skills bring good to communities and the planet? What are the needs around you that aren't being fulfilled? What if you could help even one homeless person find permanent housing?

What is Act 3 of life—this period from 60 to 90 years old? It's many things—a time of new freedom to fully be ourselves; a time of review and reflection. We're two-thirds of our way through life. We start to realize, "Hey, my time comes *now* or not at all." It's now or never. Tell yourself you intend to live happily ever after.

It's time for some soul-searching to determine what's important to you; what to do with your time to maintain your health, friends, family, and/or social groups. Studies have found the more you plan and think ahead, the more likely you are to enjoy a happy retirement. Otherwise, your golden years may not be so golden after all.

Chapter Eleven

The Quest for Happiness:
Are We There Yet?

You don't always enter wow years in perfect shape, but what matters most is how you handle disappointment, heartbreak, trauma, and crisis. Denise, now in her early sixties, lived a charmed life for most of her adult life. She has been a successful speaker, best-selling author of numerous books, and an executive coach, and lives in a beautiful place overlooking the water in California. This past year, she was called upon to help her adult child through a life-threatening experience, which culminated in her taking custody of her teen grandson while also caring for her 90-year-old mother. Meanwhile, the deep, committed relationship she had been in for several years came to a close. She couldn't help but wonder, *I've come all of this way and life decides to throw me a curve like this now?*

Denise faced heartbreak and major crises with courage and amazing self-care. Heartache can actually bring on physical stress responses, such as chest pain, insomnia, body aches, and feelings of nausea.

Denise knew it was vitally important to maintain her health and well-being while healing her heart. Following these life-changing events, she took an intensive seminar in living from the heart, established a new fitness regime, took online courses in personal growth, worked with a highly skilled therapist, daily spent time with good friends, meditated, made new friends, listen to cutting-edge podcasts, journaled her feelings daily, spent time in nature daily, and started a weekly spiritual study group that met at her place.

Along with that, she initiated going through the Conscious Uncoupling process with her partner, so that both of them could move on with clarity and no regrets.

Denise stepped up her game and truly is a role model for handling traumatic events in her wow years with grace. She now has a plethora of new people, places, and opportunities on the horizon, and says it's how one re-writes his or her life script that counts the most. She's ready to share her newly transformed, empowered life, manifest the biggest love of her life, and continue her dream of transforming the world in every way she can.

At this stage in your life, you've weathered a lot of life's ups and downs, suffered some heartbreaks, hopefully gained some wisdom, gained resilience—and the good news is, believe it or not, that the odds are now in your favor for these coming years to be the happiest of your life. Statistics now back this up. Sociologists have consistently conducted more than 50,000 interviews since 1972 for the General Social Survey, a survey conducted by the National Opinion Research Center at the University of Chicago. The survey compared differently-aged individuals over time within the same year, and researchers found that happiness increases with age.

I have noticed that most of my friends and family, aged 65 to 85 and beyond are much more content with their lives. They are able to dip into the toolbox of social and emotional skills they've gained with life experience. Even our intimate relationships can actually be better as we age.

My sister, Jo calls this time in her life her "grace period." She says her 70's are truly a time of grace. After climbing the mountains, she's now enjoying the view, reflecting and savoring moments with her husband and friends. She has more flexibility and time to volunteer, to call someone or reach out to people.

"Not only did researchers find that older people tend to be happier, but that happiness is not something older participants had all their lives. In other words, as people get older—say starting at age 50—happiness comes to them...An *aging* America may be the *happiest* America we have ever seen. Perhaps this is because of the wisdom that comes with age, or because older people adjust their expectations in life, but whatever the reason, there is solid evidence that older Americans are truly happier than younger ones."

While we can acknowledge truth in these findings, as we can see from Denise's story, happiness doesn't just happen by default. You still need to be an active participant in creating a joyful, happy mindset and plan this next wow chapter of your life. The most powerful action you can take is to set your intention to be happy and simplify your life by making this singular act your primary quest. A quest is defined as a pursuit; a long or arduous search for something; a goal or target attempt to achieve something difficult. Is the quest for happiness truly arduous? For some who don't equate passion with happiness, the question "What are you passionate about?" can be a great challenge. When you get an idea at least three times and it won't dissipate, take note of it. Watch for signs, clarification, and synchronicity that edges you towards happiness. What are the longings you have repressed thus far in your life? Listen to the whispers of your intuition. In the past, you may have been so intent on making a living, moving up in your career, raising children, and establishing a firm financial foundation that you didn't have time to think too much about your unique happiness quest. You may have felt overwhelmed by all the problems in the world; you so badly wanted to make a difference and yet you were trying to keep your head above water, dealing with all your own personal challenges.

Happiness can be rooted in understanding who you are now *being*. What is your desired outcome today, tonight, the from next 20 to 30 years? Your thoughts, feelings, and desires are all connected like a web; a matrix to the quantum field. These threads are invisible but are they ever *real!* If you add excitement and feeling to what you want, the manifestation will work like magic. Napoleon Hill said,

> "Desires that are mixed with emotional feeling magnetize the brain cells in which they are stored and prepare those cells to be taken over and directed by the law of hypnotic rhythm. Thoughts, when they are mixed with the keen emotional feeling of desire stimulate the law of hypnotic rhythm which begins at once to translate it into is physical counterpart." Outwitting the Devil (Napoleon Hill)

As Neuroscientist and author, Dr. Joe Dispenza says, "Thoughts that fire together wire together."

I saw a lot of corporate meanness in past jobs; a mean-spirited workplace. I saw really good people treated shabbily, getting laid off due to corporate greed. These environments made it challenging to find happiness or feel empowered to have a personal quest. Like so many baby-boomer women my age (raised in the 1970s, '80s, and '90s), I was a pioneer entrepreneur when I decided to get out of the corporate world and make it on my own. We didn't have many female role models in business. I had a woman boss who was basically trying to be a duplicate version of a man. I then hesitantly became the boss when she left the company and eventually became an entrepreneur/business owner almost by default. When my former corporation pressed me heavily with rising sales quotas and then reneged on the cruise I validly won, I devised an exit strategy then and there. I evaluated all the burned-out workers I had spent time with and decided to create a company that would serve the purpose of relaxation and rejuvenation for burned-out people. My vision was to be creative, independent, and represent spa resorts that would help transform people's lives, so *voila*—I founded Elite Resorts & Spas. Sometimes, the only way to find it is to create it yourself.

In his book, *The Happiness of Pursuit*, Chris Guillbeau reveals how anyone can bring meaning into his or her life by undertaking a *quest.* Chris spoke with strivers and saw the direct link between questing and long-term happiness. He explained how going after something in a methodical way enriches our lives. He interviewed hundreds of questers, such as people personally identifying every bird species on the planet, people walking across America for a cause, or people like himself; he visited every country on Earth—193 United Nations member states.

My methodology was to implement some of the same teachings I had been given since childhood, including to-do lists my dad taught me when I was ten. To-do lists have been an excellent tool in helping me accomplish my goals. They say successful people write down their goals. HuffPost reported that Dr. Gail Mathews, a psychology professor at the Dominican University in California studied the art and science of goal setting. She discovered that those who wrote down their goals and dreams on a regular basis achieved those desires at a significantly higher level than those who did not. She found that you become 42% more likely to achieve your goals and dreams simply by writing them down on a regular basis.

Speaking of writing down goals on pen and paper versus laptop, I recently attended a high-tech conference in Los Angeles with cutting-edge speakers and was taking notes in a small journal. A 25-year-old techy guy next to me looked over and said "Wow, cursive!" He was commenting on the fact that I was actually still writing in long hand. He looked at me like I was writing hieroglyphics or something. Wikipedia describes cursive as "longhand, script, handwriting, looped writing, joined up writing, running writing; written in a conjoined and or flowing manner; generally for the purpose of making writing faster."

I said, "Why is that so strange? Don't you write in cursive anymore?" He said, "No. It's not even being taught anymore. We just type or print." He looked at me like I was a dinosaur; a replica from days gone by. Although many of my friends and colleagues just text and type on laptops, I actually still enjoy putting pen to paper, journaling, and taking notes in long hand. Like the authors, J.K Rowling and Wayne Dyer, I write more creatively and easily in longhand. It just feels more personal, pouring out my thoughts and feelings onto paper. Even if you're a big fan of typing, how about occasionally substituting your laptop for a paper and pen? Studies suggest that:

1. cursive is better for learning
2. it makes you a better writer
3. it will prevent you from being distracted
4. it keeps your brain sharp as you get older (Chris Gayomali)

There are even neurological benefits to using paper and pen to write down thoughts, from the brain down the arm to the hand to the page, in regards to the retention factor.

Even when you write affirmations, cursive is connected to the subconscious mind, so writing them in cursive connects your positive affirmations to your subconscious mind. They say it goes from your brain, down your arm, to your hand, onto the page, and there's actually power in the pen.

The bridge: building your wow years

How can you start a whole new chapter? How can you take work you're now doing and incorporate it into the pursuit of your quest? How do you now follow more of your passions? By leaning in; many people in their fifties and sixties are like me. I could have kept playing the corporate game, but I just didn't want to do it anymore. I've noticed many people in their fifties become consultants in their specific fields. I leaned into the new career. I started a whole new chapter when I built my business leading people to resorts and spas for rejuvenation. Luckily, I worked in a home office, so when I was leaning in, I would work from 9am to 2pm for my main, corporate job and from 2pm to 5pm for my new career. I had come from corporate America and was burnt out. Whether you are pushed out the door of a corporate job or you leave on your own, it's important not to romanticize the move. We all need to pay the bills, so you have to be strategic and practical. It must be done carefully, with commitment, energy, and discipline. I was a self-starter, but I still needed the support of my mastermind group, friends, family, and cheerleaders. I would ask myself this Stephen-Covey question almost every day, "What can I do today towards what matters most in my life?" Know thyself. I had a flexible schedule but maintained a structure. I'd schedule power walks with good friends, and social activities for later.

Just as I had leaned into my company, Elite Resorts & Spas when I was 50 years old, in my sixties, I leaned into my new career as a certified professional coach, certified seminar leader, keynote speaker, and workshop leader. I had coordinated and taught group retreats and workshops at beautiful resorts as a side career for 18 years and I now decided I wanted to teach and coach full time. I took writing classes in the evenings for five years and focused on writing essays, which evolved into this book. I've always been a curious person with a passion for reading cutting-edge, motivational, self-help books and online courses about subjects like the new breakthroughs in neuroscience. I love sharing powerful tools that help others manifest the life of their dreams.

Balance

I knew I had a lot of life experiences, yet in forming both companies, I often went towards my fallback position of workaholic. I would forget to focus on having a great relationship or happy, fulfilling marriage, and then after a seventeen-hour workday, wonder why I am eating dinner all alone. Instead of beating myself up for my ambitions and conditioning, I acknowledge there will be setbacks, sadness, and letdowns, even this late in life. We are always learning, and it never stops.

Action step

What's going right? Are you an unrelenting taskmaster who is too hard on yourself? Look back over your calendar and your journal for the past year and acknowledge your *wins* and accomplishments. I love to do this, especially in Late December; I go through my calendar for that recent year and write a list of all my *wins* for the past year. I marvel and express gratitude for all the blessings and all that went *right*. It's important be grateful; to tell yourself how far you've come and how well you've done. Pat yourself on the back regularly, especially when you work from home and don't have a real boss. I always tell friends that one of my arms is longer than the other from patting myself on the back so often.

You can even use your iPhone calendar to review your year, make more reminiscent notes (under the "Notes" section of the calendar) about how you met someone, or career benchmarks before they get erased from the phone. Your soul feels so nurtured by recognizing your progress. Also, having a coach or a mentor in your life who acknowledges your progression when you can't see it is really important, especially if you work for yourself. Look how far you've come.

Work on your mindset. Make a commitment to a positive change today that is a non-negotiable. Commit to living your best chapter ever. If you don't feel that, then go back and read this again. *No* excuses! A great start would be committing to meditate every day. The mindset piece is everything.

Another way to lean into your new business or cause in your wow years is to run two businesses simultaneously. In 2009, after the economic downturn, many people had been laid off or fired, and at 50 years old or older, they *had* to reinvent themselves. I noticed when I'd go to business networking events and receptions that more and more people had two separate business cards. One card might be their event-planning company and the second card might be their sales representative business—selling organic, cosmetic products. The reasons for their two businesses might be financial necessity, passion for the product, burn out, desire to improve their quality of life, or spend more time with their children. You don't have to quit cold-turkey and start driving Uber, but it does take some strategy.

If you have a stable income in one job, you can move towards your budding, new field by offering your services in your new area of interest without charging a fee. I have hosted and facilitated complimentary Heart-to-Heart, Hospitality-Salon discussion evenings in San Diego, Orange County, and Los Angeles for the past five years and they've been very successful. We gather hospitality industry professionals every other month in the evening with the goal to network, come from the heart, express ourselves, discuss current issues, and help each other. We discuss subjects like mindfulness in the workplace, navigating change, electronic overload, and more. These events are personally rewarding, they support my coaching business, and help me network and meet more potential clients, so they're really a win-win.

When do we ever *get there*? Do we ever realize we've arrived? Where is "there" anyway? Someone keeps moving the finish line forward.

The quest is part of the traveling. The journey can often be better than the arriving; it's the quest that brings meaning and satisfaction to life. While on a quest, it's also vital to sit back, take a deep breath, and savor the moment. If not, you will be so consumed by the quest for happiness that the results themselves will be lost in the flurry of action. Here, where you are, is "there." I've had fleeting moments over the years when I've felt like I was "there"—a yacht trip in the Virgin Islands, visiting some amazing resorts and chateaus in Napa, wine tasting, hosting my family at my home for a barbeque on a warm summer day with our favorite songs playing in the background, meditating in my backyard secret garden with birds chirping and fountains flowing, enjoying dinner and conversations with close family and friends who love me, sitting on the beach on Catalina Island and looking out at the glistening water. I strive to have more moments like these and really sink into them as part of my wow quest.

Loving and valuing yourself

I know, I know—every self-help book preaches to the same choir; love yourself. I like to look at self-love from a different angle. I choose to recreate in higher regard. I am recreating *me* in higher regard. You can recreate you. You are not finished or complete. Life is hardly over. For many people with a quest for happiness and fulfillment, life is just beginning. That can seem daunting at an older age, but we know so much; we have an incredibly large bag of tools and tricks to apply to our wow quest.

What would it feel like to know you are enough? Feeling a sublime appreciation for your life; to feel like you *have* actually made it. There is more right than wrong with you. You are making peace with the now, focusing on how far you've come, rather than how far you have yet to go. Maybe you actually *have* arrived. Hmm…are you there, after all: right here, right *now*?

Action step

Are you there yet? We very often go through life with these goals; one year, five years; yet we never take the time to pause and realize how far we've come. Even if to this point you have not set goals, make a list of everything you have accomplished, seen, or done, and then see how that feels. How about letting out a big sigh, exhaling, and saying, "Ahh! I've finally arrived."

What about this radical thought? Imagine if your goal is to not set goals anymore but to explore what brings you happiness and follow that path? Is *that* when you'll know you've arrived to the place you want to be?

You can narrow down your re-creation into more specifics. I like the way I am as a loyal and trustworthy partner. You are calling in a person who gets you, either as a romantic relationship, business partnership, or friendship. You can start to be free to no longer hold back behaviors or opinions that may carry some kind of shame or judgment. You have acquired these judgments of yourself in some of your corporate job environments, old religious programming, toxic romantic relationships, or the way you were parented. It's time to let them go.

How do you continue on your quest when it gets too daunting? Get yourself into the mindset of being open to receive ideas and inspirations, even if they may scare you. When you take this a level higher, you are opening to the magic in your life. I accomplish this mindset by bringing white light to a situation. The results are always better than I expected. I send white light or God's loving energy to a person, asking for the highest good, before I meet with them. This practice always elevates the

TAKE A MOMENT, BEFORE
MEETING, EATING, MOVING

135

meeting in some way, and I make lasting friends. I met an executive at NBC in Burbank after I sent white light to the luncheon, and she has been a client and dear friend over the course of 30 years.

I also fortify the wow quest by laying a prayer field, which is similar to sending white light, before I meet with someone, especially if they're going through a difficult time. You're taking the meeting up to a higher level and letting spirit move through you. We are here to bring the higher realms into human form and work through our life that way. While the quests for happiness are for us, we also need to be of service to others to have life balance. When we are in the mindset of surrender and trust in divine order, life unfolds perfectly.

I was hit in traffic the other day. The woman, Lisa who hit my car from behind and scratched my bumper was actually a really nice person and a dog walker. I told her I know a detailer, Jose, who could repair the damage to my car very affordably. She paid $150 for the car to be re-detailed. The car detailing ended up only costing $100, so he didn't know how to refund her. He ended up going over to her house, washing, and detailing her SUV too. She said "Oh that is so kind; my car is so full of dog hair. Thank you so much!" We made what could've been a contentious, time-consuming problem into a friendship circle. I was also willing to refer her to someone who needs a dog walker. Life is so funny when you are open. Crazy, I actually made a new friend that day. Lisa is now my wonderful, new cat sitter when I go on trips, who sends me videos of my cat and does a great job.

Action step

Create an action plan for the next year. A helpful format is provided below. Once you've written out your goals for Act 3 and identified your quest, it's time to create a new program and fully commit to creating your best chapter ever—your wow years.

Action Step Worksheet

DATE _____

WORK/CAREER   COMPLETION DATE

_____   _____
_____
_____   _____

Examples: Research two types of jobs online and read job descriptions.
Update my resume and send out to three jobs.
Schedule one "field research" meeting to learn more about a specific job.

PHYSICAL/HEALTH   COMPLETION DATE

_____   _____
_____
_____   _____

Examples: Find a walking partner to walk with once or twice a week.
Lose five pounds; Stop eating sugar; Join a gym or YMCA.

PERSONAL/SPIRITUAL/SELF-NURTURE   COMPLETION DATE

_____   _____
_____
_____   _____

Examples: Take a bath in Epsom salts and light a candle.
Do something NEW and BRAVE every day.
Buy myself flowers.
Practice stress reduction technique (meditation) five minutes a day.

Chapter Twelve

Fully Commit to Wow Years

I NTENTIONS . .

Cynthia is a popular intuitive energy healer in Los Angeles, who I have worked with twice over the years to help her create her perfect job. She wrote out one of the most beautiful descriptions of a perfect job that I have ever seen. Her goal at the time was to do phone sessions with clients, work out of her home, and create the perfect life with her daughter and husband. She is now a highly sought-after speaker on many consciousness-raising, live radio shows that draw worldwide clients. She offers two to three big-income-producing online seminars per show. Within three years of doing the exercise with me, she was making six figures. She loved the exercise because she was able to put into words what she truly values and her career honors and affirms what she loves to do. Isn't that what we all want?

The exercise was like a roadmap to what she clearly came here to do and it was a great opportunity to reflect on her truth and the excitement of realizing her greatest dreams. Cynthia put a lot of description and energy into her visualization of how she saw herself. It reminded her that what you want really does want you. She wrote an incredible story that helped her hone-in on *why* she is here—to create heaven on earth and help fulfill humanity's highest truth of bringing its divinity into its every-day world. She really focused on the visualization and affirmations, and the exercise took her from the cosmic level down to earth with practical steps to manifest her vision for humanity. She worked on valuing her self-worth and addressed her underlying fears, since she knew that the outer world is a reflection of our inner state of mind and heart. The whole world has opened up to Cynthia. Her advice? She says, "Don't settle for something that doesn't serve the world. Identify, claim, and master your greatness in a way that is perfect for you. Serve in a way that originates from your heart and brings satisfaction to you, and it will serve others in the way it was meant to. Become a role model for others to do the same. Listen to your inner guidance. Dare to be different and dare to be your greatest self. Put your trust in your own divine truth and know that your heart and soul will lead you to exactly where you need to be in the world."

In order to have wow years, my wish is that you too will create a new program from the teachings in this book. Each exercise and action step are key ingredients for manifestation. As we discussed in chapter six, release any old, default program that life is a struggle. Once you have identified old patterns that are no longer working for you, create and recommit to your new go-to programs. Decide that this is an amazingly awesome and easy time of life, full of magic and wonder. When someone fully commits, the world opens up.

A client was married to a man who was very stingy with his time and money. He had ample savings but would never travel with her. She longed to see the world. He smoked and drank too much and died of cancer in his fifties. She entered her wow years determined to meet someone who was generous and adventurous. She is now remarried to a man who loves to travel, and she's finally happy, exploring the world with her new husband. Good for her! Pondering her story really made me ask, if not now, when? Will I ever go after the list I keep deleting? Instead of getting overwhelmed and giving up, you can prioritize the list so you actually chip away at it. I like to call this playing Intendo.

Play Intendo: What are your intentions for the next 10 years?

Here's an exercise I do in my journal about once a month. I write, "The highest and best I want to feel, be, do, have, and experience." Here are some examples:

- Experience my best, most satisfying love relationship ever
- Make a positive impact for animals and the environment
- Learn to meditate deeper and longer to fully connect to my divine source
- Post my blog regularly with helpful tips
- Publish a best-seller
- Teach more empowerment workshops that truly stretch people to their maximum potential
- Work with a powerful group of high-vibe, solution-based people, and really make a big positive difference in the world
- Tell my family and friends—while they're alive—how much I love them and why
- Rent a house on the beach for my whole family
- Be fully present with people
- Become a brilliant, inspiring speaker
- Write a TED Talk and deliver it
- Acknowledge/compliment others on their efforts and good qualities
- Heal any disagreements or unfinished business
- Travel to Australia, New Zealand, and the South Pacific

I work on all these goals today as if I could leave this earth tomorrow. I remind myself that the moment counts more than plans for tomorrow, so act. No one promised us tomorrow, but now is a gift; act on it.

Fully commit to your goals now. Let's say you live another 30 years—the next 10 years seem like they will be the most crucial in terms of health, energy, and vitality. Let's say, while I am not trying to be a downer, that 30 years is really only five years; there's nothing wrong with having a sense of urgency. Intend to accomplish your goals and be aware of finding balance in your life now. Appreciate nature, exercising, spending quality time with friends and family, enjoying hobbies and free time, making a living, and paying the bills. It's all possible.

Meditating will create short-cuts to what you want in life. Make it a non-negotiable part of your day. Every day I meditate flows *so* much better than days when I don't. Listen to that still voice within. Without a doubt, your inner world greatly affects your outer world. When you're exhausted and stressed out, imagine meditation as cleaning the dirt off your windshield or the dust off a lightbulb; it helps you see life with more clarity.

"Meditation helps you get into the flow like riding on a wave of light" (Diana Loomans).

Think back on the wide-eyed idealist you were in your twenties. You had such pure, hopeful, high, lofty dreams. You are still that person; only a lot wiser. It's harvest time. Pick all your best fruits and take some steps towards fulfilling these dreams now.

Steve Jobs was an idealist who changed the world. He never took "no" for an answer and he changed the way the world communicates, interacts and entertains. He even changed the way we think. He definitely had regrets and felt he hadn't always been there for his children. In his later years he wanted them to know why and to understand what he did. Even Steve Jobs' last words were "Oh wow. Oh wow. Oh wow." It makes you wonder what wows he experienced in those last moments.

You were born for a purpose. Never lose faith in what you can do as a human being. You too can change the world in your own way. What is *your* purpose?

Give yourself that wow-feeling of wonder, delight, and amazement at the end of a day. You know the feeling—you tried something you'd never done before. Gulp! You were scared, but you stepped up bravely and did it. You stuck your neck out and it worked. You shake your head in awe and say to yourself, "Damn, I *did it*. Wow! It all unfolded perfectly. Who knew?" No matter what age you are now, today can be the turning point of your life and guess what—this is it—these *are* your wow years *now!*

Action step

What would you regret not doing if your life here on Earth was to end soon? Take some time to reach deep within yourself to answer these questions They are big ones. Write down your thoughts.

Is there someone you need to forgive? Is there someone who needs to forgive you? Ask for forgiveness.

Do you need to apologize to someone or several people? It's an elephant off your chest. Don't be afraid to be vulnerable. It takes courage to be vulnerable.

Are you still holding any grudges? Let's call this catch and release.

Do you have any petty quarrels that need some healing and TLC?

How much energy do you use up when you're at odds with someone?

Is there an old, deep, hurt that keeps coming up and making you sad?

Has the time come to shine a light on it, get some counseling, write about it, clear it, heal, and let it go?

Is there something you've been saying you want to do for years now?

"What do you plan to do with your one, wild, and precious life?" (Mary Oliver).

It's time to play Intendo!

Intendo

Today's date_____

My Intention: _____

Example: <u>To live the most fulfilling, awesome chapter of my life *ever!*</u>

Write down ten intentions for the next ten years, or even twenty intentions for 20 years. Remember to align your intentions, thoughts, feelings, and emotions.

I (your name), _____fully commit to making these (my wow years) transformative, joyful, and my best ever!

My wow years

Directions:

1. Write your top 10 (or even 20) intentions of what you would like to manifest in your life and *be grateful for them in advance.* Write them as if you have already received them, not as if you will have them in the future. (Be specific.)
2. After each item, write *why* I'm grateful for it.
3. **Read each of the items on the list in your mind or out loud every morning. After each item, say "Thank you, thank you, thank you."**
4. *Visualize* yourself already having each of the items; the more detailed the visualization the better. Mentally rehearse the scenes.

5. Attach *feeling* to each of them. Feel as you would feel when each is a reality. Feel the happiness, thrill, joy, serenity, etc. The goal is for you to have the *CHILL FACTOR* every time you visualize them.

My word(s) for this decade:

_____

Examples: manifestation, expansion, peace, enchantment, magic, fulfillment, love, etc.

My wow-years' intentions

I'm thankful in advance that...

(I've included some examples to get you started. Feel free to make any changes according to your personal intentions. This is about you and what YOU want!)

1. I attracted _____
   Why: This is such an important part of life; this deeply enhances every aspect of our lives.
2. I transitioned to _____
   Why: I make a positive difference in the world to help raise consciousness and empower people to help them live their most awesome chapter ever.
3. I am making $_____or saving $_____ this year and even have some other new avenues of income.
   Why: I can live with comfort and ease and give to all my causes.
4. I travel with my friends, spouse or partner to _____
   _____
   _____
   Why: I'm excited to see the world with my loved ones and learn about other cultures.
5. I now have a great relationship with _____ and love deepens and grows each year. _____

_____

_____

Why: I always wanted to have this type of loving, harmonious relationship.

6. I weigh _____ pounds easily and consistently and am proud to be a slim, healthy person. I exercise several times a week, have excellent posture, and am in fantastic physical shape. _____

_____

Why: It's so easy to look fantastic and stay fit and slim for the rest of my life. This is my new *go-to* weight.

7. My _____ and I share hobbies, social events, volunteer projects, read together, play together.

_____

_____

Why: We enhance one another's lives and are both the happiest we've ever been. This spreads out to the world.

8. I'm happy and blissful, using my talents, making a positive difference in the world.

_____

_____

Why: It's my legacy to the world. It's so fulfilling.

9. _____

_____

Why: _____

_____

10. _____

_____

Why: _____

_____

New archetypes

When we are rushing around, we often don't take time to talk to older people who may have the infinite wisdom we are looking for. Some may be passing into a more quiet, soulful stage of their wow years, and are now simply aged; however, not all people are this way. There is a new group of well-known unstoppable octogenarians, as mentioned in an article by Jan Etherington—Clint Eastwood, Jane Fonda, Robert Redford, Gloria Steinem, Joan Collins, Sir Michael Caine. "Not a creaky geriatric among them, they are without exception smart, curious, interested in everyone and everything...and still working. They are in demand not because they are old but because they are still fascinating us and we want to see and hear what they have to say. Age has certainly not withered them." On the contrary, they've been invigorated by their life experience. The list of active, dynamic 80-plus-year-olds in this new paradigm goes on: William Shatner, Willie Nelson, Gene Hackman, Ruth Bader Ginsburg, Jon Voight, Joyce Carol Oates, Ruth Bader Ginsburg, Governor Jerry Brown, Julie Andrews, James Earl Jones, Sean Connery, Maggie Smith, and Judi Densch. Age is a state of mind. If you think you are old and frail, you will act as if you're old and frail—busy with new projects, onto the next page. It will be said about me, "She's great, for any age."

They have "lived a grand lifetime, left behind an immense legacy, and still find the energy to be awesome today" (*The Coolest Celebrity Octogenarians,* Ranker).

My father, Dr. John (Jack) Connor, who was 92 years old in 2007, had his wits about him until his dying day. He felt a person was never too old to realize a new goal or dream. He wrote seven books in the last 15 years of his life. He was an extraordinarily complete human being. He was infinitely curious. He had a sharp mind, strong will, and was still conversing, sincerely interested in his family and many friends of all ages until his last breath.

"In everyone's life, at some time, our inner fire goes out...It is then burst into flame by an encounter with another human being" (Albert Schweitzer).

Once, I was waiting at a bus stop in Vancouver, British Columbia with my sister, Shirley, and we started chatting with a lovely, petite, elderly woman. After a while, she shared with us she was a survivor of the Titanic. Amazing! Here was one of the last living survivors of the Titanic that sunk on its maiden voyage. She recounted her incredible experience of that historic tragedy as our jaws dropped in surprise. What other stories are we missing by rushing past each other? Keep that in mind as you walk through life. The other day, my next-door neighbor, Riah, who is retired, gave me a generous gift card with a note that said, "Thank you for always being such a great neighbor!" I wondered what I did to deserve such a wonderful gift. I casually chat with her every so often across the wall between our driveways and always love to hear about her husband and children. I guess I had just been there for her.

Action step

How can you practice presence, show sincere interest in a neighbor, a stranger, or a friend, and rekindle the flame in someone's inner spirit today? The next time you see an older person, say hello, pause to take an interest in them, and watch their eyes light up.

You can't rush the process of the wow years. Can you think back to the weeks or days *before* you got the fantastic job offer that changed your life, or the weeks *before* you met the love of your life? Yes, it was frustrating, but all those lessons—those other job interviews, those stepping-stone relationships, the so-

so or almost-right dates—helped you know when you were finally offered the perfect job or meeting "the one." Can you actually take some deep breaths, suspend judgment, and be content with *now*? Enjoy the richness of each step of the journey with childlike wonder. Shift to gratitude; trust. Miracles *are* actually unfolding. Now is a precious moment. I look back on the times I cried for what I didn't get; the cheating boyfriend I wanted to marry but didn't (dodging a bullet); the house I wanted to buy, didn't get, but then found one much better; the jobs I didn't get before the perfect job offer came my way; temporary let-downs, pain, and challenges that turned into huge blessings in the end. My greatest traumas often turned into deep lessons and lasting blessings. So, it was actually divine delay; God's delays were not God's denials.

Action step

Can you accept and become ok with where you are right now?

How is what you're going through possibly perfect for what you came here to do?

What are you learning? What is seeking to emerge? How are you changing?

How have your life experiences prepared you for what you still long to do?

This is a period where it's important not to just jump at every opportunity that comes your way. Check in with your intuition; your inner wisdom. Can you remember a time where you did *not* listen to your intuition and you made a poor decision?

Can you recall a time where you really listened to your intuition and ultimately made the perfect decision?

Beyond your empty nest, beyond your career transitions, the divorce, illness, death of a loved one, these wow years will continue to surprise you. Look at this time with childlike fascination.

What are the needs around you that aren't being fulfilled? That which wants to happen through you is itching to happen in the world. It could be the next big thing or something small and simple, but important to you. It's a time of recalibration. What do you *really* want now? Our most important desires nurture our souls. Allow divine spirit to work through you and take you to your ultimate wow—your higher purpose. What are your natural talents, passions, and interests? Those are indications of your divine life purpose. Make a difference in someone's life today. Tell someone why you love him or her. Go for that job you never thought you would get, or go back to school and earn your master's or PhD. What are you waiting for? I'm making a commitment to bring more wow into my life every day. To feel something I've never felt before, I must *do* something I've never done before and then *voila!* I'll boldly become someone I've never been and was always meant to be. I intend to live bigger, give bigger, and love bigger.

I intend to live my wow years to my fullest capacity.

Will you join me?

"If not us, then who? If not now, then when?" (John E. Lewis).

Dorthy Rose Sarah Bobby
Mary
1909   Lillian
                    Peasant
                    Stock   Toots — 1910

Hadi   Max   Molly   Reuben
 ↓   ↓   ↓   ↓
Pneumonia Womanizer   N. H.   Deserts
                              Esther   Family

                              No Kids
                              Lost Baby

→ Disabled.
  "Fear"
                                        Gamblers, Addiction
  "Worries"   Also Parent.

Eating → Obesity Plague??   → Also Parent.

        ↓
    Hostess
    Family
    Lord Hosting

        Power to Heal
    Past Present & Future

About the Author

During her hospitality industry career working in corporate America, Rita Connor represented some of the top Four- and Five-Star resorts and hotels in the world. In the year 2000, Rita's passion for the transformative powers of spa resorts inspired her to create her own successful company, Elite Resorts & Spas, where she promoted meetings and incentives to some of the finest, independent hotels and resorts in North America.

In Rita's Act 3, she became a Licensed Professional Coach, Author, Certified Seminar Leader and Keynote Speaker. She also leads retreats and workshops, sharing cutting-edge insights about Your Wow Years. Rita specializes in guiding people and sharing tools to supercharge their second half of life. She resides in Redondo Beach, California.

310-379-4295

rita@yourwowyears.com

www.yourwowyears.com

I am so grateful that
I have been able to share
the oneness of the Universe
Thank you thank you
thank you.

Made in the USA
Lexington, KY
06 July 2019